Frederick P. Buttell
Michelle Mohr Carney
Editors

Women Who Perpetrate Relationship Violence: Moving Beyond Political Correctness

Women Who Perpetrate Relationship Violence: Moving Beyond Political Correctness has been co-published simultaneously as *Journal of Offender Rehabilitation*, Volume 41, Number 4 2005.

More pre-publication
REVIEWS, COMMENTARIES, EVALUATIONS . . .

"The overview and review of the literature by Dutton and colleagues is quite good. There is a good discussion of clinical implications and a very thorough list of published work in this area."

Bonnie E. Carlson, PhD
Professor, School of Social Welfare
University at Albany
State University of New York

"PROVOCATIVE. . . . INDISPENSABLE for those who want to learn about the under-reported problem of domestic violence perpetrated by women as well as all of those who deal with cases of domestic violence. Dutton and his associates in British Columbia offer an outstanding review of the small but important literature on female perpetrators of intimate abuse. Other chapters trace the phenomenon of women as aggressors in intimate partner homicides. Another compares male and female recidivism rates."

Leon Ginsburg, PhD
Visiting Professor
California State University
Northridge; Visiting Professor
University of Southern California

Women Who Perpetrate Relationship Violence: Moving Beyond Political Correctness

Women Who Perpetrate Relationship Violence: Moving Beyond Political Correctness has been co-published simultaneously as *Journal of Offender Rehabilitation*, Volume 41, Number 4 2005.

Monographic Separates from the *Journal of Offender Rehabilitation*

For additional information on these and other Haworth Press titles, including descriptions, tables of contents, reviews, and prices, use the QuickSearch catalog at http://www.HaworthPress.com.

The *Journal of Offender Rehabilitation*™ is the successor title to the *Journal of Offender Counseling, Services & Rehabilitation*,* which changed title after Vol. 15, No. 2, 1990. The *Journal of Offender Rehabilitation*™, under its new title, begins with Vol. 16, Nos. 1/2, 1990.

Women Who Perpetrate Relationship Violence: Moving Beyond Political Correctness, edited by Frederick P. Buttell, PhD, and Michelle Mohr Carney, PhD (Vol. 41, No. 4, 2005). *"The overview and review of the literature by Dutton and colleagues is quite good. There is a good discussion of clinical implications and a very thorough list of published work in this area." (Bonnie E. Carlson, PhD, Professor, School of Social Welfare, University at Albany, State University of New York)*

Rehabilitation Issues, Problems, and Prospects in Boot Camp, edited by Brent B. Benda, PhD, and Nathaniel J. Pallone, PhD (Vol. 40, No. 3/4, 2005). *"A well-researched, well-written, and well-presented collection of chapters by the leading experts on the subject. Required reading for policymakers and scholars interested in discovering what works (and what doesn't) in corrections. This book collects some of the best and most recent empirical research on boot camps, along with several excellent summaries of the extant research. It is timely, thought-provoking, and a major contribution to the literature on correctional treatment." (Craig Hemmens, JD, PhD, Chair and Professor, Department of Criminal Justice Administration, Boise State University)*

Treating Substance Abusers in Correctional Contexts: New Understandings, New Modalities, edited by Nathaniel J. Pallone, PhD (Vol. 37, No. 3/4, 2003). *"Intriguing and illuminating. . . . Includes qualitative and quantitative research on juvenile and adult-oriented programs in the United States, Britain, and Hong Kong. . . . Examines a multitude of issues relevant to substance abuse treatment in the criminal justice system. . . . Also includes several chapters examining the effectiveness of drug courts. . . . Provides some answers to the questions being asked about RSAT programs and highlights what may be the most intriguing and encouraging development in corrections in the past quarter-century. I highly recommend this book to anyone interested in substance abuse treatement programs." (Craig Hemmens, JD, PhD, Chair and Associate Professor, Department of Criminal Justice Administration, Boise State University)*

Transcendental Meditation® in Criminal Rehabilitation and Crime Prevention, edited by Charles N. Alexander, PhD, Kenneth G. Walton, PhD, David Orme-Johnson, PhD, Rachel S. Goodman, PhD, and Nathaniel J. Pallone, PhD (Vol. 36, No. 1/2/3/4, 2003). *"Makes a strong case that meditation can accelerate development in adult criminal populations, leading to reduced recidivism and other favorable outcomes. . . . Contains original research and reviews of over 25 studies that demonstrate the effectiveness of TM programs in criminal rehabilitation." (Juan Pascual-Leone, MD, PhD, Professor of Psychology, York University)*

Religion, the Community, and the Rehabilitation of Criminal Offenders, edited by Thomas P. O'Connor, BCL, BTheol, MS, and Nathaniel J. Pallone, PhD (Vol. 35, No. 3/4, 2002). *Examines the relationship between faith-based programs, religion, and offender rehabilitation.*

Drug Courts in Operation: Current Research, edited by James J. Hennessy, PhD, and Nathaniel J. Pallone, PhD (Vol. 33, No. 4, 2001). *"As one of the founders of the drug court movement, I can testify that Dr. Hennessy's book represents the highest level of sophistication in this field." (Michael O. Smith, MD, Director, Lincoln Recovery Center, Bronx, New York; Assistant Clinical Professor of Psychiatry, Cornell University Medical School)*

Family Empowerment as an Intervention Strategy in Juvenile Delinquency, edited by Richard Dembo, PhD, and Nathaniel J. Pallone, PhD (Vol. 33, No. 1, 2001). *"A hands-on book. . . .*

Provides detailed guidelines for counselors regarding implementation of the FEI curriculum . . . accurately describes the scope of counselor responsibilities and the nature of treatment interventions. Unique in its coverage of counselor competencies and training/supervision needs. Innovative and based on solid empirical evidence." (Roger H. Peters, PhD, Professor, University of South Florida, Tampa)

Race, Ethnicity, Sexual Orientation, Violent Crime: The Realities and the Myths, edited by Nathaniel J. Pallone, PhD (Vol. 30, No. 1/2, 1999). *"A fascinating book which illuminates the complexity of race as it applies to the criminal justice system and the myths and political correctness that have shrouded the real truth. . . . I highly recommend this book for those who study causes of crime in minority populations." (Joseph R. Carlson, PhD, Associate Professor, University of Nebraska at Kearney)*

Sex Offender Treatment: Biological Dysfunction, Intrapsychic Conflict, Interpersonal Violence, edited by Eli Coleman, PhD, S. Margretta Dwyer, MA, and Nathaniel J. Pallone, PhD (Vol. 23, No. 3/4, 1996). *"Offers a review of current assessment and treatment theory while addressing critical issues such as standards of care, use of phallometry, and working with specialized populations such as exhibitionists and developmentally disabled clients. . . . A valuable addition to the reader's professional library." (Robert E. Freeman-Longo, MRC, LPC, Director, The Safer Society Press)*

The Psychobiology of Aggression: Engines, Measurement, Control, edited by Marc Hillbrand, PhD, and Nathaniel J. Pallone, PhD (Vol. 21, No. 3/4, 1995). *"A comprehensive sourcebook for the increasing dialogue between psychobiologists, neuropsychiatrists, and those interested in a full understanding of the dynamics and control of criminal aggression." (Criminal Justice Review)*

Young Victims, Young Offenders: Current Issues in Policy and Treatment, edited by Nathaniel J. Pallone, PhD (Vol. 21, No. 1/2, 1994). *"Extremely practical. . . . Aims to increase knowledge about the patterns of youthful offenders and give help in designing programs of prevention and rehabilitation." (S. Margretta Dwyer, Director of Sex Offender Treatment Program, Department of Family Practice, University of Minnesota)*

Sex Offender Treatment: Psychological and Medical Approaches, edited by Eli Coleman, PhD, S. Margretta Dwyer, and Nathaniel J. Pallone, PhD (Vol. 18, No. 3/4, 1992). *"Summarizes research worldwide on the various approaches to treating sex offenders for both researchers and clinicians." (SciTech Book News)*

The Clinical Treatment of the Criminal Offender in Outpatient Mental Health Settings: New and Emerging Perspectives, * edited by Sol Chaneles, PhD, and Nathaniel J. Pallone, PhD (Vol. 15, No. 1, 1990). *"The clinical professional concerned with the outpatient treatment of the criminal offender will find this book informative and useful." (Criminal Justice Review)*

Older Offenders: Current Trends, * edited by Sol Chaneles, PhD, and Cathleen Burnett, PhD (Vol. 13, No. 2, 1985). *"Broad in scope and should provide a fruitful beginning for future discussion and exploration." (Criminal Justice Review)*

Prisons and Prisoners: Historical Documents, * edited by Sol Chaneles, PhD (Vol. 10, No. 1/2, 1985). *"May help all of us . . . to gain some understanding as to why prisons have resisted change for over 300 years. . . . Very challenging and very disturbing." (Public Offender Counseling Association)*

Gender Issues, Sex Offenses, and Criminal Justice: Current Trends, * edited by Sol Chaneles, PhD (Vol. 9, No. 1/2, 1984). *"The contributions of the work will be readily apparent to any reader interested in an interdisciplinary approach to criminology and women's studies." (Criminal Justice Review)*

Current Trends in Correctional Education: Theory and Practice, * edited by Sol Chaneles, PhD (Vol. 7, No. 3/4, 1983). *"A laudable presentation of educational issues in relation to corrections." (International Journal of Offender Therapy and Comparative Criminology)*

Women Who Perpetrate Relationship Violence: Moving Beyond Political Correctness

Frederick P. Buttell
Michelle Mohr Carney
Editors

Women Who Perpetrate Relationship Violence: Moving Beyond Political Correctness has been co-published simultaneously as *Journal of Offender Rehabilitation*, Volume 41, Number 4 2005.

The Haworth Press, Inc.

New York • London • Victoria (AU)
www.HaworthPress.com

Women Who Perpetrate Relationship Violence: Moving Beyond Political Correctness has been co-published simultaneously as *Journal of Offender Rehabilitation*, Volume 41, Number 4 2005.

The development, preparation, and publication of this work has been undertaken with great care. However, the publisher, employees, editors, and agents of The Haworth Press and all imprints of The Haworth Press, Inc., including The Haworth Medical Press® and Pharmaceutical Products Press®, are not responsible for any errors contained herein or for consequences that may ensue from use of materials or information contained in this work. With regard to case studies, identities and circumstances of individuals discussed herein have been changed to protect confidentiality. Any resemblance to actual persons, living or dead, is entirely coincidental.

The Haworth Press is committed to the dissemination of ideas and information according to the highest standards of intellectual freedom and the free exchange of ideas. Statements made and opinions expressed in this publication do not necessarily reflect the views of the Publisher, Directors, management, or staff of The Haworth Press, Inc., or an endorsement by them.

Cover design by Jennifer M. Gaska

Library of Congress Cataloging-in-Publication Data

Women who perpetrate relationship violence : moving beyond political correctness / Frederick P. Buttell, Michelle Mohr Carney, editors.
    p. cm.
    "Co-published simultaneously as Journal of Offender Rehabilitation, Volume 41, Number 4 2005."
    Includes bibliographical references and index.
    ISBN-13: 978-0-7890-3130-3 (hard cover : alk. paper)
    ISBN-10: 0-7890-3130-2 (hard cover : alk. paper)
    ISBN-13: 978-0-7890-3131-0 (soft cover : alk. paper)
    ISBN-10: 0-7890-3131-0 (soft cover : alk. paper)
    1. Abusive women. 2. Family violence. I. Buttell, Frederick P. II. Carney, Michelle Mohr. III. Journal of offender rehabilitation.
  HV6626.W65 2005
  616.85'822'0082–dc22
                            2005019554

Indexing, Abstracting & Website/Internet Coverage

This section provides you with a list of major indexing & abstracting services and other tools for bibliographic access. That is to say, each service began covering this periodical during the year noted in the right column. Most Websites which are listed below have indicated that they will either post, disseminate, compile, archive, cite or alert their own Website users with research-based content from this work. (This list is as current as the copyright date of this publication.)

(continued)

(continued)

Special Bibliographic Notes related to special journal issues (separates) and indexing/abstracting:

- indexing/abstracting services in this list will also cover material in any "separate" that is co-published simultaneously with Haworth's special thematic journal issue or DocuSerial. Indexing/abstracting usually covers material at the article/chapter level.
- monographic co-editions are intended for either non-subscribers or libraries which intend to purchase a second copy for their circulating collections.
- monographic co-editions are reported to all jobbers/wholesalers/approval plans. The source journal is listed as the "series" to assist the prevention of duplicate purchasing in the same manner utilized for books-in-series.
- to facilitate user/access services all indexing/abstracting services are encouraged to utilize the co-indexing entry note indicated at the bottom of the first page of each article/chapter/contribution.
- this is intended to assist a library user of any reference tool (whether print, electronic, online, or CD-ROM) to locate the monographic version if the library has purchased this version but not a subscription to the source journal.
- individual articles/chapters in any Haworth publication are also available through the Haworth Document Delivery Service (HDDS).

Women Who Perpetrate Relationship Violence: Moving Beyond Political Correctness

CONTENTS

ABOUT THE EDITORS

Frederick P. Buttell, PhD, is Associate Professor in the School of Social Work at Tulane University in New Orleans, Louisiana. His primary research interests and expertise are in the areas of batterer interventions, research methods, and quantitative data analysis. Dr. Buttell has extensive clinical experience in providing court-mandated treatment services to batterers and he has investigated numerous aspects of batterer intervention programs. He has served as a training consultant to the Alabama Coalition Against Domestic Violence and the Women's Center at the University of Alabama and has evaluated aspects of service provision for male and female batterers. He teaches courses on advanced clinical practice and family development.

Michelle Mohr Carney, PhD, is Associate Professor in the School of Social Work at the University of Georgia in Athens, Georgia. Her primary research interests and expertise are in the areas of delinquent youth and batterer interventions, and evaluation research. She has conducted several evaluation studies, including evaluations of service provision for male and female batterers. She teaches graduate courses in macro practice (especially foundation and advanced community practice, development and non-profit administration), evaluation research, and case-based integrative seminars.

This volume is dedicated to Dr. Nathaniel Pallone, who had the wisdom to see the truth about domestic violence and the courage to challenge our beliefs about it.

Women Who Perpetrate Relationship Violence: Moving Beyond Political Correctness. Pp. xv-xvii.
Available online at http://www.haworthpress.com/web/JOR

Foreword

In the mid-1990s, we were providing clinical services to batterers in a court-mandated batterer intervention program (BIP). As mandatory arrest laws swept the nation, we, like clinical service providers everywhere, discovered that a significant portion of our court referrals were women (i.e., 25%). In our quest to discover how to treat this population of women arrested, prosecuted and convicted of domestic violence offenses, we went to the literature. Interestingly, we discovered that the literature was replete with articles addressing women as victims, but very few articles dealt with the construct of women as offenders. Consequently, with no good studies to guide us otherwise, we simply plugged these women into the same program we had created for male batterers. Recent history has taught us that this was not a novel solution, as the majority of treatment providers nationally have reported doing the same thing. Experience, however, quickly taught us that this was an idea bound for limited success, as the women in the BIP were as variable as the men.

In our experience, there were many women in our BIP who were like those described in the literature in terms of being both a victim and offender in their intimate relationships. Conversely, there was a substantial group of women in every cohort that resembled the worst of the male batterers. Specifically, this subset of women indicated that they had never been abused by their partners, had all the power in the relationship, and advocated the use of violence to maintain their power advantage. In brief, they articulated a view of relationships that was directly related to the issues of power and control addressed in intervention programs for male batterers. Not surprisingly, given the wide range of women in treatment for domestic violence offenses, there appeared to be wildly divergent outcomes. It seemed that the BIP curriculum designed for work with male batterers had a better fit for those women who were the primary aggressors in their intimate relationships. Unfortunately, for those women who were primarily the victims in their intimate relationships or were engaged in relationships characterized by bi-directional violence, the curriculum failed to directly address their experiences. Even worse was our discovery that the group experience tended to exacerbate the problems experienced by women with a history of victimization in their relationships. Specifically, when placed in a group with women who were the primary aggressors in their intimate relationships, women who occupied the dual status of victim and offender felt demeaned by the more aggressive women, who frequently commented that they "would never be treated like that" and that these women were "weak." As a result, the group experience was, at best, rocky and uneven, but there was no discussion of how to address any of these issues in the professional literature.

Although ten years have elapsed, we still know very little about domestically violent women. Recent studies have indicated that, like domestically violent men, there are subtypes of domestically violent women. However, compared to the voluminous literature on male batterers, knowledge about female batterers is in the embryonic stage. Although there are many possible explanations for this situation, it has been our experience that political correctness is the primary culprit. We have had articles addressing aspects of female initiated violence rejected for the most spurious of reasons (even when they were largely identical to accepted articles that addressed male initiated violence). For years, we have talked with colleagues at conferences in hushed whispers about the problems we have discussed above, but only in hallways and out of earshot of other attendees, whom we didn't know. The purpose of this special issue is to strip away political correctness and take a frank look at the issues surrounding female violence in intimate relationships. Contributors were instructed to be brutally honest in their appraisal of what the issues were and to write candidly about their chosen topics. At the end of the day, we believe we have created something meaningful that will advance the knowledge base surrounding domestically violent women. Don Dutton, Tonia Nicholls and Alicia Spidel have provided us with an elegant and concise review of the literature on women who are violent in their intimate relationships. In our article, we extend Dutton's idea of the abusive personality to female batterers by exploring issues of attachment and dependency among domestically violent women attending a court-mandated BIP. Victoria Titterington and Laura Harper explore gender and racial differences in homicide rates, while Brian Renauer and Kris Henning investigate who is more likely to recidivate, men or women, following an arrest for domestic violence. Finally, Catherine Simmons, Peter Lehmann, Norman Cobb, and Carol Fowler investigate personality characteristics of domestically violent women and compare them with domestically violent men. For this special issue, our goal was to move beyond political correctness and assemble the most current research on women who batter. We feel strongly that this issue focuses on women as the perpetrators of domestic violence–not victims, and captures the most recent ideas and research on the topic.

Michelle Mohr Carney
University of Georgia
School of Social Work

Frederick P. Buttell
Tulane University
School of Social Work

Women Who Perpetrate Relationship Violence: Moving Beyond Political Correctness. Pp. 1-31.
Available online at http://www.haworthpress.com/web/JOR
doi:10.1300/J076v41n04_01

Female Perpetrators of Intimate Abuse

DONALD G. DUTTON
TONIA L. NICHOLLS
ALICIA SPIDEL

ABSTRACT A review is made of female intimate abuse. It is concluded that females are as abusive as males in intimate relationships according to survey and epidemiological studies. This is especially so for younger "cohort" community samples followed longitudinally. Predictors of intimate violence with women appear to be similar to those of men; including antisocial criminal records, alcohol abuse, and personality disorders. *[Article copies available for a fee from The Haworth Document Delivery Service: 1-800-HAWORTH. E-mail address: <docdelivery@haworthpress.com> Website: <http://www.HaworthPress.com> © 2005 by The Haworth Press, Inc. All rights reserved.]*

KEYWORDS Female batterers, domestic violence

Compared to the extensive literature on male perpetrators of intimate abuse (Dutton, 2002; Hamberger & Hastings, 1991; Holtzworth-Munroe, Bates, Smutzler, & Sandin, 1997, inter alia), the literature on female perpetrators is scant. Although it has long been recognized that North American women and men are equally likely to be the perpetrators or the victims of intimate abuse (Steinmetz, 1977; Straus & Gelles, 1992), in large part, this knowledge has been prevented from influencing public policy and informing interventions for couples coping with violence in their relationships. For years, the dominant feminist view in intimate violence research precluded the reporting of female battering (see Straus & Gelles, 1992, pp. 3-16) or dismissed it as merely self-defense (Dobash & Dobash, 1978, 1979; Dobash, Dobash, Wilson, & Daly, 1992). As a result, until very recently, political correctness and concerns that reports of female perpetrated abuse might decrease funding and other sources of support for female (i.e., the only) victims of partner violence have successfully silenced publications of such findings (e.g., see Felson, 2002) and, unwittingly, prevented progress in successfully preventing and treating this widespread public health issue.[1]

It likely would not be an overstatement to suggest that an important evolution is occurring in the domestic violence field. First, scholars are increasingly asserting that violence in relationships needs to be considered within the larger context of interpersonal violence and that focusing our attention on correlates and motives known to predict general violence can inform our understanding of violence between intimate partners (Dutton, 1994; Dutton & Nicholls, in press; Felson, 2002). In direct contrast to the traditional radical feminist perspective, the emerging generation of research literature asserts that partner abuse reflects intimacy, interpersonal conflict, psychopathology, and demographic and psychosocial correlates common to other areas of criminology and forensic psychology (e.g., prior antisocial and violent behaviors) (Dutton & Nicholls, in press; Ehrensaft, Moffitt, & Caspi, 2004; Felson, 2002). Second, women's perpetration of abuse and men's victimization experiences in intimate relationships are emerging as important considerations in safety planning, preventive and therapeutic interventions, and legal responses to domestic violence. Although the work of Straus and colleagues awakened the field to women's use of abuse tactics in relationships long ago (Steinmetz, 1977; Straus & Gelles, 1992), it has taken decades for the realities of those innovations to begin to be reflected in public policy and used to inform evidence-based practice. It is against this backdrop that we will examine women's use of abuse in intimate relationships and begin exploring the treatment needs of women who engage in abuse against their partners.

ABUSE PERPETRATED BY WOMEN AGAINST MALE INTIMATE PARTNERS

There is no shortage of discussion in the literature regarding the controversial issues of who hits first, who hits more often, and who presents a *real* threat of harm to their partners, men or women? Recent empirical and theoretical reviews (Archer, 2000, 2002; Dutton, 1994; Dutton & Nicholls, in press; Felson, 2002; Fiebert, 2004; George, 1999, 2003; Nicholls & Dutton, 2001; Straus, 1999) provide compelling evidence that the rates of victimization and perpetration are similar among men and women in intimate relationships and the severity of violence and resulting harm is most often minor (Dutton, 1998; Ehrensaft et al., 2004; Johnson, 1995; Makepeace, 1986). Furthermore, evidence is amassing that contradicts the notion that women's aggression is primarily in self-defense against abusive male partners.

Similar Rates of Victimization and Perpetration Among Men and Women

Over the past few decades, a growing number of studies have been released that support the contention that females perpetrate violence at rates equal, or similar, to males (for reviews, see Dutton & Nicholls, in press; Fiebert, 2004; Straus, 1999). Findings are relatively consistent across dating, cohabiting, and marital relationships in community samples; though, there is some evidence to suggest young respondents (under 30 years) in dating relationships evidence higher rates of aggression, particularly by women (Follingstad, Wright, Lloyd, & Sebastian, 1991; Sommer, Barnes, & Murray, 1992; Sorenson, Upschurch, & Shen, 1996).

More than two decades ago, Bernard and Bernard (1983) surveyed 168 males and 293 females enrolled in introductory psychology courses, 30% of the students reported having abused a partner or having been abused by a partner. Fifteen percent of the men reported they had victimized a partner, of those male abusers 77% reported they also had been abused. Of the women, 21% reported they had perpetrated abuse and, of those, 82% also had been victimized. Around the same time, Henton, Cate, Koval, Lloyd, and Christopher (1983) sampled male and female high school students and demonstrated that 78 (29 males and 49 females) of the original sample of 644 reported having been the aggressor or the target of physical violence in a dating relationship. Henton and colleagues concluded that the abuse could most commonly be characterized as reciprocal; 71.4% of respondents reported that they had been both the victim and the aggressor at some point during the relationships.

A few years later, O'Keefe, Brockopp, and Chew (1986) surveyed 135 female and 121 male high school students. The results indicated that the prevalence of violence did not differ significantly by sex: 11.1% of females and 10.7% of males reported being victimized, without having perpetrated violence. Burke, Stets, and Pirog-Good (1988) sampled 505 (298 females; 207 males) upper-class students from a large midwestern university. The results indicated no significant differences in men's and women's reported perpetration and victimization rates; 14% of men and 18% of women in their sample engaged in physical violence against a date; 10% of men and 14% of women reported having been physically assaulted by a date. Thompson (1991) provided data from a sample of 336 undergraduates, which further indicated that physical aggression in dating relationships is not gender specific. The use of any form of aggression in the context of a dating relationship in the two years prior to the study was reported by 24.6% of the men and 28.4% of the women (Thompson, 1991).

More recently, Magdol et al. (1997; also see Moffitt, Robins, & Caspi, 2001) conducted one of the few prospective studies to examine the prevalence of violence in intimate relationships. These investigators followed a birth cohort of 1,037 subjects in Dunedin, New Zealand. At age 21, 425 women and 436 men who were in intimate relationships from the Magdol et al. cohort answered Conflict Tactics Scale (Straus, 1990) questions about their own and their partners' use of violence. Both minor and severe physical violence rates were higher for women, whether self or partner reported. The female severe physical violence rate was more than triple that of males (18.6% vs. 5.7%). Stranger violence was also measured and again was more prevalent among women (36% vs. 25%).

In a sample of 70 male undergraduates who were unmarried and had been in a dating relationship in the last year, Simonelli and Ingram (1998) found that 40% reported on the CTS (Straus, 1979) that they had been the victim of at least one violent act in the past year. Twenty-nine percent reported that they had been the victims of severe violence (e.g., kicked, bitten, hit with a fist, had a gun or knife used against them). In comparison, 10% of the men reported that they had used severe violence against a partner.

Nicholls, Desmarais, Spidel, and Koch (2005) compared the prevalence and nature of victimization and abuse perpetration in a sample of undergraduate men ($n = 13$) and women ($n = 52$) from a mid-sized Canadian university who had been in heterosexual relationships for at least three months. As anticipated, results from the CTS2 (Straus, Hamby, Boney-McCoy, & Sugarman, 1996) indicated lifetime victimization and perpetration of abuse in intimate relationships among undergraduates was common and differed little by the gender of the respondent. With regard to perpetrating abuse, none of the comparisons between men and women for the prevalence of the various categories of abuse on the CTS2 reached significance. Women had somewhat higher rates of perpetration across all categories of abuse (psychological, physical, sexual coercion, injury) regardless of the level of severity considered (i.e., any, minor, or severe on the CTS2); with the exception of men being somewhat more likely to report having committed minor sexual coercion (38.5%) than women (23.1%). Undergraduate men and women also generally reported similar rates of victimization: psychological abuse (women = 78.8%; men = 69.2%), physical abuse (women = 26.9%; men = 23.1%), and sexual coercion (women = 42.3%; men = 46.2%). There was some evidence the women were more likely to have experienced serious abuse. Results indicated severe psychological abuse (women = 32.7%; men = 38.5%), severe physical abuse (women = 11.5%, men = 0%), severe sexual coercion (women = 15.4%, men = 7.77%), any injury (women = 9.6%; men = 0%) and severe injury (women = 1.9%, men = 0%) occurred in a substantial minority of undergraduate relationships and tended to be somewhat more likely to be experienced by women than men.

Community research with participants in marital or cohabiting relationships reveals similar evidence of gender symmetry in abuse perpetration and victimization. Kwong, Bartholomew, and Dutton (1999) surveyed a representative sample of 356 men and 351 women from the province of Alberta. Regardless of the gender of the respondent they found similar one-year prevalence rates for husband-to-wife violence, with men reporting slightly higher rates (not significant). Men and women also agreed on the prevalence of wife-to-husband violence.

Using U.S. national survey data, Stets and Straus (1990) demonstrated that women were three times as likely to use severe violence against a non-violent male partner than were men against a non-violent female partner. For reasons that may have to do with the predominant view of family violence as male perpetrated, this important finding has largely gone unnoticed. Unilateral female violence ranged from 9.6% in married couples to 13.4% in cohabiting couples (the comparable rates for male unilateral violence were 2.4% and 1.2%) (Stets & Straus, 1990). Hence, female violence could not be characterized as solely self-defensive. Archer's (2000, 2002) meta-analytic study of gender and violence usage in intimate relationships revealed females, if anything, were somewhat more violent than males, according to summed self/other reports.

Only in "crime victim" surveys, do men still appear as the more frequent perpetrators of intimate aggression; scholars propose this might reflect differential definitions of crime, demand characteristics of the surveys, and/or sensitivity to detection (Archer, 2000; Dutton & Nicholls, in press; Straus, 1999). Furthermore, males report being injured by female partners at a rate more similar to female injury rates than feminist reports have reflected (Archer, 2000). The injuries are frequently obtained by female use of weapons to physical attacks on male genitalia (Hines, Brown, & Dunning, 2003; Morse, 1995).

Evidence That Women Aggress Against Non-Abusive Partners

As we have demonstrated, many studies ascertain that women commit partner violence at similar or higher rates than males. A limitation of gender symmetry identified by many critics is that women's aggression might be in self-defense; less commonly asserted, but possible, is that some men might similarly be aggressing against their partners in response to female initiated aggression. Contrary to the self-defense hypothesis, several authors have reported that many women who use violence report striking the first blow. In a Canadian sample, Bland and Orn (1986) reported that of the women in their sample who used violence against their husbands, 73.4% said they used violence first. Similarly, Stets and Straus (1992) reported that women committed the first act of aggression more than half of the time (52.7%). In a large sample of American dating college students ($N = 968$ women) Fiebert and Gonzalez found 29% of women revealed they initiated assaults.

Further research also provides evidence that women aggress against non-abusive male partners. Lewis, Travea, and Fremouw (2002) assessed variables associated with female violence in dating relationships in a sample of 300 undergraduate women. They found that 16% of the women engaged in bi-directional violence and 7% of the women were the sole perpetrators of abuse (69% were in non-violent relationships, 8% were victims). In 1998, Majdan surveyed 103 female undergraduate students currently involved, or involved in the last year, in a heterosexual dating relationship of at least one-month duration. Majdan determined that women reported engaging in more psychological and physical aggression than they reported experiencing. The prevalence of physical assaults perpetrated by the women was higher for both prior year (44%) and lifetime (49%) than the prevalence of physical victimization reported by the women (36% and 41%, respectively). The prevalence of abuse perpetrated by the women that resulted in injuries in the last year and over their lifetimes were identical (11%); they were also comparable to the prevalence of abuse that resulted in injuries to the women in the last year (11%) and over the women's lifetimes (15%). Majdan (1998) reported that the women experienced more sexual coercion (36% last year; 39% lifetime) than they perpetrated (25% last year; 27% lifetime).

In a sample of 505 Caucasian undergraduate women Stets and Pirog-Good (1987) reported the women were more likely to experience and to use violence in a dating relationship than men; however, the differences were not significant. Stets and Pirog-Good (1987) proposed that women may be more likely to report violence than men (note that the rate of violence experienced by women is fairly equivalent to the rate of using violence by men). However, it may be that the women were involved in mutually abusive relationships–which would explain why both the rate of female abuse and use of violence was higher for the women in this sample than for the men. In their undergraduate sample, Simonelli and Ingram (1998) found that men were more likely to report being seriously victimized than to report having inflicted serious harm on their partners.

Undergraduate men and women in the Nicholls et al. study reported comparable rates of abuse perpetration and victimization on the CTS2. Men reported similar prevalence rates when asked about perpetrating psychological abuse (69.2%), physical abuse (30.8%), sexual coercion (38.5%), and injuries (0%) as when they were asked about those types of victimization experiences (69.2%, 23.1%, 46.2%, 0%, respectively). Women also reported perpetrating psychological (86.5%), physical (38.5%), sexual coercion (44.2%), and injuries (11.5%) at a rate similar to their rates of victimization across those same categories (78.8%, 26.9%, 42.3%, 9.6%, respectively). Although it cannot be ascertained from that study whether respondents' partners were abusive or not, it is instructive to note the women were slightly more likely to report perpetrating each form of abuse than they were to report victimization in each category. These findings have made it increasingly difficult to view abuse in intimate relationships as solely, or even primarily, a reflection of sexism, misogyny, or patriarchy.

Reporting Issues

Considerable criticism has also been leveled at gender symmetry findings in the partner abuse literature from the perspective that there may be reporting issues to be considered. Most commonly, the assumption seems to be that men underreport their use of abuse against their partners and overreport their victimization experiences (Bernard & Bernard, 1983; Dobash et al., 1992). The veracity of women's reports of victimization tend to come under much less scrutiny. Women's reports of abuse are generally taken at face value (also consider reports of sexual harassment, childhood sexual abuse, and rape) (see Dutton & Nicholls, in press; Felson, 2002; Henning & Feder, 2004). In fact, men and women in Henning et al.'s (2003) study were equally likely to respond on the MCMI-III in ways to make them look favourable.

Contrary to the hypothesis that men exaggerate their victimization experiences evidence suggests men are unlikely to report abuse experiences due to socio-historical influences (e.g., gender-role socialization). Burke and colleagues (1988) pointed to the disparity between the number of men who reported having been physically assaulted and the number of women who reported committing physical assault, suggesting that perhaps males underreport physical victimization by female partners because it is considered "normal" or not recognized as "violence" per se.

In one of the more influential examinations of the reporting issue, Straus and Gelles (1992) broke down violence rates on the basis of who did the reporting. The largest discrepancy was for males under 25 years of age to underreport wife violence compared to wives' reports of their own violence. Husbands' reports of their own victimizations were only 72% of wives' perpetration reports for all assaults. Conversely, husbands' perpetration reports were 79% of wives' victimization reports (p. 553). *Wives' perpetration reports were 208% of husbands' victimization reports. Men grossly underreported both perpetration and victimization by severe violence.*

A review of the literature indicates that like men, women initiate abuse, women commit unilateral aggression (i.e., against non-abusive partners), sometimes of a serious nature, and the majority of abusive relationships involve mutual abuse; the evidence is broadly consistent, regardless of the gender of the respondents (Dutton & Nicholls, in press; Ehrensaft et al., 2004).

Severity of Abuse of Abuse Perpetrated by Women

It has been suggested that the severity of abuse and the negative physical, psychological, and financial implications of abuse suffered by men is not comparable to that experienced by women (Saunders, 1988). Considerable research confirms that an important minority of women suffer egregious harm as a result of chronic severe abuse by a small proportion of men (Dutton, 1998; Walker, 1984); that does not, however, preclude the possibility that men might also suffer serious harm as a result of severe abuse by female (or male) partners (Dutton & Nicholls, in press). A brief review of the literature suggests that on average women sampled from the community commit serious violence against their male partners at rates that rarely differ significantly from male perpetration rates of severe violence.

In 1991 Thompson reported that women committed more severe aggression than men. Although the differences were not significant, 7.2% of the men and 10.7% of the women reported that they had used severe aggression against a date and 13.8% of men and 8.9% of women reported they had been severely victimized by a date. Similarly, Magdol et al. (1997) asserted that the female severe physical violence rate was more than triple that of males (18.6% vs. 5.7%). Stranger violence was also measured and was again more prevalent by women (36% vs. 25%). Kwong and Bartholomew (1998; also see Kwong, Bartholomew, & Dutton, 1999) found that women who were victimized were about twice as likely to report severe injuries (14% vs. 7%) and to feel physical pain the next day (38% vs. 18%) than men who were victimized. These "effect" data were for the percentage of *victims* who experienced injury or pain. When calculated as a percentage of the entire population, the results indicated 2.5% of men and 4% of women had severe injuries, 6.5% of men and 11% of women experienced physical pain.

Ridley and Feldman (2003) examined 153 volunteer females from a community public health clinic in a study of conflict and communication. The women in their sample reported the following physical abuse frequencies directed at their male partners: kicking, 20.2%, choking/strangling, 9.1%, physically attacking the sexual parts of his body, 7.1%, using a knife or gun against him, 7.8%. Women who engaged in these acts reported using them repeatedly (i.e., 40 incidents of kicking [per perpetrator who reported using this action], 6.5 incidents of "physical attacks to the sexual parts," 4.25 acts of choking per perpetrator, etc.).

In a sample of female undergraduates who admitted to committing partner abuse on the CTS2 (Straus et al., 1996) Spidel, Nicholls, and Kropp (2003) reported that although most of the abuse was minor (71%) (items 1-10), moderate (26%) (items 11-14) and severe (3%) (items 15-19) abuse was not uncommon. Furthermore, evidence suggests that men victimized by their female intimate partners do experience serious harm. For instance, in a study of dating violence among high school students, Callahan, Tolman, and Saunders (2003) found increasing violence was related to PTSD and dissociation among females and predicted anxiety, depression, and PTSD among the male respondents, even controlling for demographic, family violence, and social desirability items.

A select review of the literature demonstrates that women use acts of abuse across the entire continuum of domestic violence identified in the literature. Consistent with research with male perpetrators of partner abuse, the bulk of women's abuse is minor but the research suggests a minority of women commit severe acts of aggression and women's abuse can result in significant negative outcomes for male victims. The impact of women's abuse on male partners is a relatively unexplored area worthy of further investigation.

ABUSE PERPETRATED BY WOMEN IN HOMOSEXUAL RELATIONSHIPS

Further evidence of women's use of abuse in relationships, men's risk for victimization by intimate partners, and data to refute patriarchal explanations of partner abuse to the exclusion of other theories, has been gleaned from research on homosexual male and female relationships (Island & Letellier, 1991; Renzetti, 1992). Lie and Gentlewarrier (1991) surveyed 1,099 lesbians, finding that 52% had been a victim of violence by their female partners. More than half the women said they had used violence against a female partner, and 30% said they had used violence against a non-violent female partner. In a CTS study of 48 lesbians and 50 gay men, self-selected for the research, Kelly and Warshafsky (1987, as cited in Renzetti, 1992) found that 47% of the sample had used physical aggression against an intimate partner.

Brand and Kidd (1986) surveyed 75 heterosexual women and 55 homosexual women, the sample consisted of mostly well-educated, middle to upper class, Caucasian women. Most subjects were students at a women's college in Northern California. Other respondents included members of a lesbian discussion group and women who answered a newspaper ad. The women responded to a 24-item questionnaire. Results indicated the rate of physical abuse reported by lesbians (25%) and heterosexual women (27%) in intimate relationships was comparable. Four (7%) of the heterosexual women reported being the victim of a completed rape and three (5%) homosexual women reported an attempted rape by a female partner in a dating relationship. Lie, Schilit, Bush, Montagne, and Reyes (1991) similarly illustrated abuse rates were higher in lesbian relationships than in heterosexual relationships. In a survey of 350 women in homosexual relationships (who had been in both lesbian and heterosexual relationships) reported rates of verbal, physical, and sexual abuse were all significantly higher in lesbian relationships than in heterosexual relationships.

Renzetti (1992) studied 100 self-identified victims of lesbian battering of whom 98% were 18-50 years old. Typical respondents in Renzetti's sample were 26-35 years old, 95% were Caucasian and the women were primarily educated–42% had graduate or professional education/degrees, only 7% were employed in blue-collar occupations, and 85% of the women were no longer in the abusive relationships. These factors reflect the lack of generalizability of Renzetti's findings, but more importantly they speak to the fact that intimate violence occurs across social classes. Renzetti concluded that situational battering (i.e., abuse that occurs once or twice while the couple is in crisis and never occurs again) appears to be relatively rare in lesbian relationships. Dependency, jealousy, imbalance of power, substance abuse, and intergenerational violence were seen as primary contributing factors to violence between lesbian partners. Fortunata and Kohn (2003) found the predictors of lesbian battering to be a history of childhood abuse, alcohol abuse and high antisocial or borderline scale scores on the MCMI-III. They concluded that psychopathological explanations best explained lesbian battering.

Reflecting on evidence of gender symmetry in perpetration and victimization rates among heterosexual couples and high rates of abuse in lesbian relationships, Dutton (2002) proposed that abusiveness was either a personality construct or else emanated from dysfunctional conflict resolution. He called for prospective studies on female abusers and argued that similar traits would be found in female abusers as were found in studies of male abusers. There is now a small literature beginning to address these issues.

CORRELATES OF WOMEN'S PARTNER ABUSE

Advancements in understanding abuse in intimate relationships have evolved almost exclusively from research exploring men's abusive or violent behaviour, women's victimization experiences, and the ensuing theoretical and treatment developments. Increasingly, it is being recognized that women's use of violence is one of the strongest predictors of their own risk for victimization (Felson & Cares, 2004). Moreover, as demonstrated above, as many as 50% of relationships involve mutual aggression and we also know that some women engage in severe violence against non-abusive men (Archer, 2000; Dutton & Nicholls, in press; Straus, 1999).

In other domains of scholarly research (e.g., violence risk assessment with female inmates/offenders and psychiatric patients) women's violence has been found to share many correlates with men's violence (e.g., substance abuse, prior violence) (Cale & Lilienfeld, 2002; Loucks & Zamble, 2000; Nicholls, Ogloff, & Douglas, 2004). That being said, there is also evidence to suggest that there may be some violence risk factors that are gender specific (e.g., gang membership), risk predictors that impact women differentially (e.g., sexual abuse, mental disorder, or intellectual deficits) (Babcock, Miller, & Siard, 2003; Hodgins, 1992), or that women's aggression might be expressed differently (Werner & Crick, 1999). Logically, then, we might expect to find that some risk factors overlap men's and women's use of aggression against intimate partners (e.g., child abuse histories, substance abuse/dependence, personality disorders, insecure attachment) but that women's intimate abuse might also stem from some unique risk predictors.

Increased knowledge of the contexts, motivations, personality characteristics, and psychosocial risk factors related to women's use of abuse and violence in intimate relationships has important implications for policy and will be useful for guiding treatment and intervention with female abusers and couples who engage in mutual abuse. Although many scholars assert women in batterer programs are likely self-defending victims (Martin, 1997) there is little research comparing the background of women receiving services for perpetrating abuse versus women in treatment as a result of suffering abuse in intimate relationships (Abel, 2001). As we have demonstrated, a large proportion of couple abuse is reciprocal, and sometimes it reflects female initiated aggression, indicating a need to explore the demographic characteristics, mental health, and criminal histories of women who commit abuse against intimate partners to better inform prevention and intervention strategies (Ehrensaft et al., 2004; Moffitt et al., 2001; Nicholls & Dutton, 2001).

Psychosocial Histories of Women Who Commit Partner Abuse

Based on his extensive review of the gender and violence literature, Felson (2002) noted delinquency and prior aggression correlate as highly with women's aggression as with men's aggression. Our review of the literature similarly leads us to conclude that women who commit abuse against their partners are a heterogeneous group, which shares many characteristics in common with male abusers and perpetrators of general violence.

Using a non-experimental design in a convenience sample, Abel (2001) compared 67 women attending a court-ordered batterer's intervention program and 51 women receiving partner abuse counselling services. Findings indicated that women in victim intervention programs were significantly more likely to be married than the women in the batterer intervention programs, who were more often dating. Both groups reported similarly high rates of victimization. There was some evidence of a trend, with batterers reporting more victim related exposures (e.g., being threatened, threats, coercive sex, etc.) though in four of the six areas of exposure the differences did not reach significance. Women in victim programs (67%) were significantly more likely to have previously used domestic violence victim services than women in batterer programs (33%).

The female victims in Abel's (2001) study reported significantly more trauma symptomology than the female abusers on the Trauma Symptom Checklist (TSC-33, Briere & Runtz, 1989). Abel did not report significance testing when comparing Briere and Runtz's non-abused women with her batterer group but TSC-33 scale and subscale comparisons for anxiety (5.73, 6.00), depression (10.10, 8.11), sleep disorder (4.35, 4.52), and overall trauma (28.25, 25.13) indicated small differences, suggesting the female batterers in this sample were similar to non-abused women in their trauma symptomology. In contrast, the women in Abel's victim programs had scores very similar to Briere and Runtz's abused group and their scores were substantially higher than Briere and Runtz's non-abused group. In addition to the lack of an experimental control and small sample size, a limitation of this study is that the "batterer" group was comprised primarily of African American women and the "victim" group was comprised primarily of Caucasian women. As the authors noted, cultural differences might have implications for help-seeking, for instance. Despite any limitations, this study provides evidence to suggest that female partner abusers are unique from female victims of partner abuse; as such, they likely present with unique treatment needs.

Holtzworth-Munroe and Stuart (1994) asserted there are three types of male batterers: family-only, dysphoric/borderline, and generally violent/antisocial. Building on their work, Babcock et al. (2003) examined the contexts and motivations of abuse reported by 52 women referred to a treatment agency for abusive behavior. They categorized the women in their sample into two a priori categories: Partner-Only (PO) women (women who reported only using aggression against their romantic partners since age 18) and Generally Violent (GV) women (women who reported using violence in a variety of circumstances since age 18). The GV women reported a mean of 7.70 ($SD = 9.21$) fights with an average of 3.58 different people. The GV women committed significantly more physical ($F(1, 50) = 8.33$, $p < .01$) and psychological ($F(1, 50) = 12.45$, $p < .001$) abuse, and also inflicted more injuries ($F(1, 50) = 5.84$, $p < .01$) against their partners during the past year than the PO women. Of note, there were no significant differences between the PO and GV groups' experiences of abuse by their partners. As the authors hypothesized, according to the Trauma Symptom Checklist (Briere & Runtz, 1989) GV women reported more current trauma symptoms than the PO women ($F(1, 50) = 3.11$, $p < .10$). The GV women more frequently reported a desire to hurt themselves, a desire to hurt others, and interpersonal problems (each at $p < .05$).

Both the GV and PO women in Babcock et al.'s (2003) sample reported high rates of childhood physical and sexual abuse. The only significant difference between the women's backgrounds was that the GV women more often reported seeing their mothers aggress against their fathers ($F(1, 58) = 8.06$, $p < .01$). Babcock et al. concluded that, similar to their male counterparts, female intimate abusers are a heterogeneous group. This study demonstrated that GV women likely have several overlapping traits with PO women but are perhaps going to present with distinctive or more extensive treatment needs.

Henning, Jones, and Holdford (2003) reported demographic, childhood family functioning, and mental health characteristics for a large sample of male (2,254) and female (281) domestic violence offenders. They found few differences between the demographic characteristics of men and women arrested for domestic violence. Women were more likely to have attended college but were less likely to work outside the home. A similar proportion of men and women had low IQs (i.e., borderline to mentally deficient) according to the WAIS-R. Analyses comparing childhood experiences that might result in adulthood adjustment difficulties or psychopathology revealed few gender differences (e.g., physical abuse, inter-parental physical aggression, parental criminal behavior, or substance abuse). Men were more likely than women to report corporal punishment by primary caregivers ($p < .01$) and women were more likely to report severe interparental abuse ($p < .01$). More gender differences were evident with regard to the subjects' mental health histories and current mental health status. The male offenders were more likely than the female offenders to report prior treatment for substance abuse/dependence, to be rated high risk for substance dependence currently, to have had childhood conduct problems prior to age 16, and to have a desire to continue the relationship with the victim. The women were more likely than the men to have been prescribed psychotropic medication and to have a prior suicide attempt. Men and women in this sample were equally likely to report clinically significant distress.

In sum, studies examining characteristics of women who commit partner abuse is a relatively novel area of research. Findings to date suggest women who are victimized by their partners can be distinguished from women who have been identified primarily/solely as abusers. Further, as we have seen from research with male abusers, women who are violent only in their intimate relationships appear to be unique from women who also commit aggression in other contexts. Finally, female abusers share many of the same traits as their male counterparts.

Psychopathology Among Women Who Commit Partner Abuse

Dutton (2002) asserted that personality factors, rather than "maleness" per se, generated emotional and physical abuse in males. In a series of empirical studies of court mandated treatment participants, Dutton showed that combinations of fearful attachment, borderline traits, and chronic trauma symptoms generated what he called an "abusive personality" in males. Recent research has begun to explore the role of these features among female perpetrators of partner abuse.

Follingstad, Bradley, Helff, and Laughlin (2002) generated a model for predicting dating violence in a sample of 412 college students. They found that anxious attachment resulting from early life experiences led to the development of an "angry temperament" which, in turn, related to attempts to control and use abuse against an intimate partner. The model predicted abusiveness for both genders.

Ehrensaft, Cohen, and Johnson (in press) followed a community sample for 20 years to study the associations among childhood exposure to family violence, personality disorder symptoms, and perpetration of intimate violence in adulthood. They found that the formation of personality disorder clusters as described in the DSM-IV mediated intergenerational transmission of family violence. Presence of personality disorder rather than gender was the better predictor of partner violence. Ehrensaft et al. also asserted that personality disorder clusters, which usually decline after adolescence, decline more slowly in abusive men and women; hence, an abusive personality appears to exist across genders. The authors described this as "having an early pre-existing pattern of distrust, interpersonal avoidance, unusual or bizarre beliefs and constricted positive affect" (p. 24). These traits remain more stable in abusive people, regardless of gender. As Ehrensaft et al. (2004) put it,

> studies suggest that this single-sex approach is not empirically supported, because both partners' behaviors contribute to the risk of clinically significant partner abuse, and both partners should be treated. Women's partner abuse cannot be explained exclusively as self-defense against men's partner abuse, because a woman's pre-relationship history of aggression towards others predicts her abuse toward her partner, over and above controls for reports of his abuse towards her. (p. 268)

Henning et al. (2003) found women arrested for domestic violence had more symptoms of personality dysfunction and mood disorders than men arrested for domestic violence. The majority of both male (64.8%) and female (67.9%) offenders had no elevated clinical scales on Axis I of the MCMI-III. Women were significantly more likely to score in the clinical range for delusional disorder, major depression, bipolar disorder, somatoform disorder, and thought disorder. Female offenders were more likely than male offenders to score in the clinical range on the MCMI-III Axis II (F (14, 1249) = 31.67, $p < .001$). Most notable, 95% of the women compared to 69.8% of the men had one or more elevated personality disorder subscales. The authors concluded that many women convicted of abuse against intimate partners are likely to have stable personality disorders that complicate their intimate relationships and are likely to have relevance to treatment.

In a recent study of female undergraduates at a large university in Western Canada, Spidel, Nicholls, Kendrick, Klein, and Kropp (2004) found a high rate of personality disorders according to self-reports on the SCID-II. In this sample of women who had committed abuse against an intimate male partner, 13.2% endorsed enough traits to meet the criterion for one personality disorder, 16.9% had two personality disorders according to their self report, and 33.1% met criteria for three or more personality disorders. The most prevalent diagnoses included Obsessive Compulsive (34.6%), Antisocial (33.8%), Passive Aggressive (28.7%), Narcissistic (22.8%), and Borderline (22.1%). Although the high prevalence rates may be due in part to self-report, the findings are in line with other samples of males who commit spousal assaults.

Magdol et al. (1997) found that perpetrators and victims of both genders presented with the same demographic profiles: unemployed (compared to non-perpetrator/victims), limited education, alcohol dependence, and high scores on mental health and criminality scales. The risk factors for female violence were high scores on a scale of psychoticism, neuroticism, and the MacAndrew Scale for alcohol abuse. Both the psychoticism and neuroticism scales as described in the study were composites of measures assessing poor ego strength and may have been correlated with borderline features in this population. Substance abuse is also a problem behavior for individuals with borderline personality disorder. Dutton's (2002) work has implicated a borderline personality structure as a risk factor for intimate violence in male perpetrators.

Carney and Buttell (2004) compared the demographic and psychological profiles of female abusers who completed treatment with female abusers who dropped out of treatment. In their sample of 50 women referred to a 16 week program for partner abuse, the authors found marital status (i.e., married [42%] vs. not married [58%]) and voluntary (22%) vs. involuntary (78%) participation in treatment significantly distinguished women who did and did not complete treatment. In contrast, psychological variables did not distinguish completers from non-completers. Of particular note, their sample of female abusers had scores comparable to a previous sample of male abusers (Buttell & Carney, 2002) on the Propensity for Abusiveness Scale (PAS) and high rates of substance use. The results lead the authors to conclude that male and female abusers present with pretreatment similarities in their use of physical violence; therefore, treatment strategies employed with male abusers might have application to female abusers, as well.

Hence, as studies begin to assess psychological factors predicting female intimate violence, a pattern similar to male violence emerges; personality disorders, especially those impacting on intimacy, attachment style, and constricted affect are all present. These manifest themselves as did the same profile in males; with an "angry temperament," substance abuse, conflict generating beliefs and intimate violence. This finding holds, regardless of whether dating violence is studied cross-sectionally, lesbian violence is studied, or longitudinal studies are done on community groups.

Women's Motivations for Partner Abuse/Contextual Variables

Findings from studies examining women's motives for using aggression mirror research comparing the prevalence and incidence of abuse by men versus women, motives and contexts reflect the sampling procedures used in the various studies. Specifically, research in female clinical samples reveals high rates of self-defense, retaliation, and aggression reportedly due to fear of impending attacks by partners that have been assaultive previously (e.g., Saunders, 1986). In contrast, data from community samples reflects more similarity in the motives underlying men and women's use of aggression, tends to contradict patriarchal explanations of partner abuse, and offers little evidence that women's aggression, on average, is primarily in self-defense.

Follingstad et al. (1991) asked victims of partner abuse about their perceptions of their assaulters' motivations and simultaneously asked perpetrators to report their own motivations for using aggression. In the total sample of 495 undergraduate subjects in South Carolina, 115 respondents (23%; 16% of the men and 28% of the women) reported a partner had physically assaulted them. Women reported being victimized and perpetrating physical aggression twice as often as men. The authors found that there was no significant difference in the percentage of men (17.7%) and women (18.6%) who endorsed using aggression in self-defense. Furthermore, a greater percentage of women than men reported using aggression to feel more powerful (3.4% vs. 0), to get control over the other person (22.0% vs. 8.3%), or to punish the person for "wrong behavior" (16.9% vs. 12.5%). The two most commonly endorsed motives by victims (i.e., their perceptions of their assaulter's motives) were not knowing how to express themselves verbally and self-defense; these were endorsed at similar rates by male victims (32.7% and 4.1%, respectively) and female victims (28.2% and 4.8%, respectively). Many views on men's abuse of women hold that the goal is control; however, this study found that few men endorsed that motive. The authors noted, while it is possible men under-endorsed this motive, the men admitted to many other socially undesirable motivations.

Babcock et al. (2003) used multiple methods to assess women's motives for using violence against intimate partners. The women in their sample reported their partners used severely violent acts at least twice as often as the women reported using severe violence against their partners. Babcock and colleagues evaluated the women's open-ended responses to the question "List your reasons for choosing violence during the incident for which you were ticketed or arrested?" Of 89 codable responses, the most common motivation was reportedly self-defense (28.3%); anger and frustration were also common (20%). The authors found no significant differences between the motives of the GV and PO women. In comparison, multivariate analyses of items on the *Reasons for Violence Scale* indicated significant differences between the GV and PO women's responses ($F (11, 40) = 2.87$, $p < .01$). Univariate analyses indicated that GV women were more likely to endorse items such as "he was asking for it" ($p < .01$), "lost control" ($p < .001$), "frustrated" ($p < .05$), and "to push his buttons" ($p < .01$). In contrast to the authors' expectations, the PO women were not more likely than the GV women to report using violence in self-defense.

The GV and PO women were also found to differ significantly on the *Proximal Antecedents of Violent Events Scale* (Babcock et al., 2003). The GV women were more likely than the PO women to use aggression as a means to control their partners ($F (1, 47) = 5.48$, $p < .01$) and were more likely to resort to using violence in response to verbal abuse or due to jealousy ($F = (1, 47) = 6.66$ and 9.91, respectively, $p < .05$ for both). There was no significant difference between the PO ($M = 7.56$; $SD = 17.38$) and GV ($M = 12.19$; $SD = 17.38$) women in the reported frequency of self-defense as a motive. The authors used multiple methods to evaluate violence committed as an act of self-defense; in some cases they failed to find a significant correlation between the methods.

Finally, there is some evidence to suggest that women's aggression is a reflection of dysfunctional attempts to establish emotional closeness to their partner. Fiebert and Gonzalez (1997) found women reported using abusive tactics to obtain their partner's attention and to attempt to engage them. Similarly, Mason and Blankenship (1987) reported female college students ($n = 107$) with high affiliation needs were most likely to be abusive to their partners. The women in Fiebert and Gonzalez's (1997) sample reported using aggression because they felt that their assaults were unlikely to result in serious harm or that their partners would retaliate. These findings suggest that interventions addressing positive communication strategies, education about the negative impacts of partner abuse on men, and the risk women's use of aggression presents for male retaliatory attacks might be effective in reducing abuse in intimate relationships.

CLINICAL IMPLICATIONS

An unintended consequence of mandatory arrest policies in many North American jurisdictions has been a dramatic increase in the number of women apprehended for abusing their partners and court ordered to attend treatment (Martin, 1997). The surge of female domestic violence offenders in the criminal justice system necessitates identifying intervention targets and developing guidelines for treating women who use abuse in their intimate relationships (Hamberger & Potente, 1994). Despite the relatively small body of literature available examining the characteristics of female abusers and predictors of women's abuse in intimate relationships, as we have demonstrated, evidence to inform clinical interventions with female abusers is beginning to mount.

Determining how best to conceptualise treatment for a female perpetrator of partner abuse should reflect evidence-based practice, a comprehensive assessment of the woman and her partner, and interviews with collaterals. Interventions that are relevant to women identified for treatment from clinical settings (e.g., women housed in shelters) likely will have similarities to strategies important to consider in treatment for women in marriage counselling and women arrested for domestic violence, but it is also possible that these heterogeneous groups will present with unique needs. As Hamberger and Potente (1994) noted, "There may be dynamics unique to non-clinical dating couples experiencing violence that do not apply to people involved in clinical treatment or intervention settings" (p. 128). They further asserted that it remains to be seen whether women who can be characterized as the primary or sole aggressor in the relationship can benefit for programs designed for women who are considered primarily victims.

Victimization Histories and Trauma Symptomology

Several authorities have focussed their recommendations for intervening with female domestic violence offenders on familial risk factors and prior victimization experiences (Abel, 2001; Hamberger & Potente, 1994; Henning et al., 2003), trauma symptoms (Abel, 2001), the oppression of women (Hamberger & Potente, 1994), and the need for safety planning (i.e., to protect the woman from her male partner) (Hamberger & Potente, 1994; Henning et al., 2003). Given high rates of victimization experiences and trauma among both perpetrator and victim groups of women in her study, Abel (2001) concluded victimization issues should be covered in curriculum offered to women involved in batterer treatment programs. Henning and colleagues (2003) similarly recommended assessing female abusers for child abuse histories and witnessing interparental abuse in the family of origin, in addition to a thorough consideration of women's mental health histories.

There likely is little doubt that prior victimization and traumas are relevant and appropriate treatment considerations–for male and female abusers, as well as male and female victims of intimate abuse. Perhaps research into treatment strategies with women who abuse their partners also will result in an increased recognition of the limitations inherent in shame-based interventions with male abusers and an increasing emphasis on social learning, psychopathology (e.g., personality disorders, attachment styles), conflict oriented theories, and related interventions. Henning et al. (2003) noted, "Traditional domestic violence programs that focus on power and control and negative attitudes toward women likely have limited utility for the female offenders" (p. 842). Recent research suggests current treatment approaches for partner abuse also have limited feasibility with male offenders (Babcock, Green, & Robbie, 2004; Babcock & Steiner, 1999; Rosenfeld, 1992).

The extant literature suggests that treating women's symptoms resulting from victimization experiences exclusively is likely to be an insufficient strategy for reducing women's use of aggression. For instance, very few of the women (5.4%) in Henning et al.'s (2003) study scored in the clinical range for Post-Traumatic Stress Disorder (PTSD). Similarly, Abel (2001) reported female offenders' trauma symptomology level was substantially lower than female victims and did not differ substantially from earlier research with non-abused women. The extent to which empowerment, safety planning, and trauma recovery are a focus of treatment with female domestic violence perpetrators should be considered on a case-by-case basis.

Responsibility, Empowerment, and Assertiveness

Although some authors have been reluctant to consider women's choices to use abusive relationship tactics, due to concerns it is tantamount to victim blaming, there is increasing consensus in the literature that women's use of aggression also can increase a woman's risk of victimization. Moreover, some experts point out that assisting women with understanding their (limited) responsibility will empower them by reducing self-defeating cognitive behavioral strategies (e.g., "I can change my partner"; "I wouldn't be able to survive without my partner") (Hamberger & Potente, 1994). Counselling around the issue of responsibility should serve to clarify that the woman is responsible for her own use of aggression and, particularly in situations involving mutual abuse, that she is not responsible for, and cannot control, her partner's behavior. Understanding violence as a choice provides the opportunity for exploring more productive problem solving strategies for managing situations that give rise to a woman's own use of abuse and/or safety planning in situations that give rise to abuse by her partner. An enhanced understanding of her responsibility should assist a woman with recognizing and implementing alternative positive behaviors for coping with tense or stressful situations with her partner and as appropriate, in other relationships or settings (e.g., parenting, in the workplace).

People who use violence tend not to feel powerful. In fact, quite to the contrary, research confirms that violent individuals often feel threatened, powerless, and fear abandonment (Estroff & Zimmer, 1994). As such, treatment programs for abusive women should foster the development of communication skills, frustration tolerance, and socially appropriate assertiveness (Hamberger & Potente, 1994).

Mood Disturbances and Personality Disorders

Women who use abuse tactics are more likely to have clinically elevated Axis I and II disturbances when compared to non-abusive women in the general population. Sommer et al. (1992) found that young women with elevated psychoticism and neuroticism scores were at greatest risk for partner abuse. Their study also indicated women's alcohol consumption might be an important consideration. Ehrensaft et al. (2004) reported that adolescent conduct disorder and aggressive personalities were present at similar rates among women in non-clinically abusive and clinically abusive relationships and distinguished women in abusive relationships from women in non-abusive relationships. Both men and women in Henning et al.'s (2003) study were most likely to be elevated on the Compulsive and Narcissistic subscales of the MCMI-III. Those authors also found women were significantly more likely than men to have elevations on the Histrionic and Borderline subscales. The authors concluded the findings suggest emotional stability and inflated self-importance should be targeted with women who use abuse in intimate relationships.

Risk Assessments with Female Perpetrators

Henning et al. (2003) reported that the women in their sample of domestic violence arrestees were less likely to have substance abuse histories and/or to be considered high risk for future substance misuse. They further found the men had higher rates of serious childhood conduct problems than the women. Henning and Feder (2004) similarly reported higher rates of adulthood criminality among male than among female domestic violence offenders. They also found male victims reported less severe abuse and less concern that their partners presented a serious threat to them than female victims. These findings resulted in Henning and colleagues (2003; Henning & Feder, 2004) concluding female abusers present less risk for future violence than male abusers. The logic in this conclusion seems inherent, however, it is based on translating templates of risk assessments for domestic violence that have grown out of work with male offenders, almost exclusively, to female offenders. It is possible, for instance, that prior conduct problems and involvement with the criminal justice system would be useful predictors for GV women but might contribute less to risk assessments with PO women (also see Felson, 2002). For instance, contrary to their expectations, Babcock et al. (2003) found the GV women in their sample were no more likely to have a criminal history than the PO women despite the fact the GV women presented a greater threat to their partners. In that study, GV women used more severe violence in a broader variety of contexts than PO women (Babcock et al., 2003). The authors noted, however, that 44% of the women in their study refused to respond to questions regarding their criminal histories.

Contrary to the assertion that female abusers present little future risk to their male partners, the Family Violence Surveys indicated that regardless of the gender of the perpetrator, if spouse abuse is reported once there is a 2/3 chance of reoffending against the partner (Straus, 1980, 1985). Similar conclusions were drawn by Ridley and Feldman (2003) who reported women who used aggression tended to use it repeatedly (two-thirds of the time). Finally, Felson (2002) concluded, "women who use violence against their husbands tend to be aggressive in other circumstances as well" (p. 211).

Henning et al. (2003) reported male and female abusers both tended to respond to Social Desirability and Validity subscales on the MCMI-III in ways intended to make them look favourable. This serves as an important reminder that forensic assessors should obtain collateral information when conducting partner abuse risk assessments (and child custody assessments) for both male and female abusers.

The validity and reliability of risk assessments with male spouse abusers is still a relatively new area with a small body of empirical evidence (e.g., Kropp & Hart, 2000). To our knowledge, little if any data on the utility of risk assessments with female spouse abusers exists. Building on the recommendations of other authors (e.g., Ehrensaft et al., 2004) we would suggest that, given that most abusive relationships involve mutual aggression, assessments in this field might often best be characterized as couples risk assessments. That being said, it is likely the approximately 9% (Ehrensaft et al., 2004) to 12% (Dutton, 1998) of relationships involving severe violence, wherein the well being and safety of one partner is the primary focus, that are most likely to be the focus of forensic evaluations.

CONCLUSION

As our discussion demonstrates, female perpetrated abuse in intimate relationships is at least as common as male abuse, often extends to the same degree of severity, can result in serious negative outcomes for male and female victims, and seems to reflect a common set of background causes. Contrary to early socio-political explanations, which proposed that women's use of aggression reflected primarily, or solely, self-defense strategies in response to male abuse, women are known to commit unilateral abuse. This suggests that many couples in treatment for partner abuse and perhaps slightly fewer who come into contact with the criminal justice system require services that address the perpetration and victimization needs of both partners. In fact, in their prospective longitudinal study in Dunedin, New Zealand, Ehrensaft et al. (2004) found that common couples abuse (i.e., non-severe abuse) was characterized primarily as woman-to-man abuse while clinically significant abuse (i.e., involving injuries and/or weapons) involved primarily mutual abuse, leading the authors to question the utility of focusing partner abuse preventions and interventions on male aggression.

Preliminary research suggests women who might best be categorized as primarily victims of partner abuse can be distinguished from women who are more appropriately categorized as primarily perpetrators. Furthermore, female domestic violence offenders share many of the same characteristics as male offenders, including similar motives and psycho-social characteristics (prior aggression, substance use, personality disturbance, etc.). Research comparing familial risk factors for intimate abuse also indicates greater similarities than differences for men and women who use abuse in relationships (e.g., witnessing interparental abuse, physical abuse by a caregiver). There is also some evidence to suggest typologies hypothesized to exist among male perpetrators might translate well to women perpetrators. Finally, research to date suggests female abusers are about as likely as male abusers to have an Axis I disorder but are substantially more likely to be in the clinical range on Axis II. In contrast, studies clearly indicate that female victims of partner abuse are not more pathological than other women, though there is some evidence they are more aggressive (Ehrensaft et al., 2004).

An improved understanding of the etiology of women's aggression has begun to shape interventions for domestically violent women. We eagerly await treatment evaluation research and are hopeful that reconceptualizing partner abuse treatment for use with female abusers will have the added benefit of challenging prevailing assumptions that men's abuse against their female partners is grown directly out of patri-archy. Abuse in intimate relationships reflects a diverse constellation of predictors. Professionals would do well to consider risk factors common to general violence when evaluating male and female abusers as well as possible intervention needs of both partners.

NOTE

1. We recognize the limited resources that are made available to provide shelter, counseling, protection, and safety planning for women with abusive male partners; we are not recommending that these services be reduced. It is essential, however, that services reflect the field's knowledge of the dynamics of partner abuse and best serve the needs of families in turmoil. The research to date suggests that a consideration of women's use of aggression will serve to reduce women's risk of victimization in addition to preventing abuse of male partners.

REFERENCES

Abel, E. M. (2001). Comparing the social service utilization, exposure to violence, and trauma symptomology of domestic violence female "victims" and female "batterers." *Journal of Family Violence, 16*, 401-420.

Archer, J. (2000). Sex differences in aggression between heterosexual partners: A meta-analytic review. *Psychological Bulletin, 126*, 651-680.

Archer, J. (2002). Sex differences in physically aggressive acts between heterosexual partners. A meta-analytic review. *Aggression and Violent Behavior, 7(4)*, 313-351.

Babcock, J. C., Green, C. E., & Robie, C. (2004). Does batterers' treatment work?: A meta-analytic review of domestic violence treatment. *Clinical Psychology Review, 23*, 1023-1053.

Babcock, J. C., Miller, S. A., & Siard, C. (2003). Toward a typology of abusive women: Differences between partner-only and generally violent women in the use of violence. *Psychology of Women Quarterly, 27*, 153-161.

Babcock, J. C., & Steiner, R. (1999). The relationship between treatment, incarceration, and recidivism of battering: A program evaluation of Seattle's coordinated community response to domestic violence. *Journal of Family Psychology, 13*, 46-59.

Bernard, M. L., & Bernard, J. L. (1983). Violent intimacy: The family as a model for love relationships. *Family Relations, 32*, 283-286.

Bland, R., & Orn, H. (1986). Family violence and psychiatric disorder. *Canadian Journal of Psychiatry, 31*, 129-137.

Brand, P. A., & Kidd, A. H. (1986). Frequency of physical aggression in heterosexual and female homosexual dyads. *Psychological Reports, 59*, 1307-1313.

Briere, J., & Runtz, M. (1989). The Trauma Symptom Checklist (TSC-33): Early data on a new scale. *Journal of Interpersonal Violence, 4(2)*, 151-163.

Burke, P. J., Stets, J. E., & Pirog-Good, M. A. (1988). Gender identity, self-esteem, and physical and sexual abuse in dating relationships. *Social Psychology Quarterly, 51*, 272-285.

Buttell, F., & Carney, M. (2002). Psychological and demographic predictors of attrition among batterers court ordered into treatment. *Social Work Research, 26(1)*, 31-42.

Cale, E., & Lilienfeld, S. (2002). Sex differences in psychopathy and antisocial personality disorder. A review and integration. *Clinical Psychology Review, 22*, 1179-1207.

Callahan, M. R., Tolman, R. M., & Saunders, D. G. (2003). Adolescent dating violence victimization and psychological well-being. *Journal of Adolescent Research, 18(6)*, 664-681.

Carney, M. M., & Buttell, F. P. (2004). Psychological and demographic predictors of treatment attrition among women assaulters. *Journal of Offender Rehabilitation, 38*, 7-25.

Dobash, R. E., & Dobash, R. P. (1978). Wives: The appropriate victims of marital assault. *Victimology: An International Journal, 2*, 426-442.

Dobash, R. E., & Dobash, R. P. (1979). *Violence against wives: A case against the patriarchy.* New York: Free Press.

Dobash, R. P., Dobash, R. E., Wilson, M., & Daly, M. (1992). The myth of sexual symmetry in marital violence. *Social Problems, 39(1)*, 71-91.

Dutton, D. G. (1994). Patriarchy and wife assault: The ecological fallacy. *Violence & Victims, 9(2)*, 125-140.

Dutton, D. G. (1998). *The domestic assault of women: Psychological and criminal justice perspectives.* Vancouver, BC: UBC Press.

Dutton, D. G. (2002). *The abusive personality: Violence and control in abusive relationships.* (2nd Edition) New York: Guilford.

Dutton, D. G., & Nicholls, T. L. (in press). A critical review of the gender paradigm in domestic violence research and theory: Part I–Theory and data. *Aggression and Violent Behavior.*

Ehrensaft, M., Cohen, P., & Johnson, J. (in press) Development of personality disorder symptoms and the risk for partner violence. *Journal of Abnormal Psychology.*

Ehrensaft, M. K., Moffitt, T. E., & Caspi, A. (2004). Clinically abusive relationships in an unselected birth cohort: Men's and women's participation and developmental antecedents. *Journal of Abnormal Psychology, 113(2)*, 258-271.

Estroff, S. E., & Zimmer, C. (1994). Social networks, social support, and violence among persons with severe, persistent mental illness. In J. Monahan, & H. Steadman (Eds.), *Violence and mental disorder: Developments in risk assessment* (pp. 259-295). Chicago: University of Chicago Press.

Felson, R. B. (2002). *Violence & gender reexamined.* Washington, DC: American Psychological Association.

Felson, R. B., & Cares, A.C. (2004). *Gender differences in the seriousness of assaults on intimate partners and other victims.* Manuscript under review for publication.

Fiebert, M. S. (2004). *References examining assaults by women on their spouses or male partners: An annotated bibliography.* Retrieved December 3, 2004, from http://www.csulb.edu/~mfiebert/assault.htm

Fiebert, M. S., & Gonzalez, D. M. (1997). Women who initiate assaults: The reasons offered for such behavior. *Psychological Reports, 80,* 583-590.

Follingstad, D. R., Bradley, R. G., Helff, C. M., & Laughlin, J. E. (2002). A model for predicting dating violence: Anxious attachment, angry temperament and a need for relationship control. *Violence & Victims, 17(1),* 35-47.

Follingstad, D. R., Wright, S., Lloyd, S., & Sebastian, J. A. (1991). Sex differences in motivations and effects in dating violence. *Family Relations, 40,* 51-57.

Fortunata, B., & Kohn, C. (2003). Demographic, psychosocial and personality characteristics of lesbian batterers. *Violence & Victims, 18,* 557-568.

Frieze, I. H. (2000). Violence in close relationships–Development of a research area: Comment on Archer (2000). *Psychological Bulletin, 126,* 681-684.

George, M. J. (1999). A victimization survey of female-perpetrated assaults in the United Kingdom. *Aggressive Behavior, 25,* 67-79.

George, M. J. (2003). Invisible touch. *Aggression & Violent Behavior, 8,* 23-60.

Hamberger, L. K. (1997). Female offenders in domestic violence: A look at actions in their context. *Journal of Aggression, Maltreatment, & Trauma, 1,* 117-129.

Hamberger, L. K., & Hastings, J. E. (1991). Personality correlates of men who batter and non-violent men: Some continuities and discontinuities. *Journal of Family Violence, 6,* 131-147.

Hamberger, L. K., & Potente, T. (1994). Counseling heterosexual women arrested for domestic violence: Implications for theory and practice. *Violence & Victims, 9,* 125-137.

Henning, K., & Feder, L. (2004). A comparison between men and women arrested for domestic violence: Who presents the greater threat? *Journal of Family Violence, 19,* 69-80.

Henning, K., Jones, A., & Holdford, R. (2003). Treatment needs of women arrested for domestic violence: A comparison with male offenders. *Journal of Interpersonal Violence, 18,* 839-856.

Henton, J., Cate, R., Koval, J., Lloyd, S., & Christopher, S. (1983). Romance and violence in dating relationships. *Journal of Family Issues, 4,* 467-482.

Hines, D. A., Brown, J., & Dunning, E. (2003). *Characteristics of callers to the domestic abuse helpline for men.* Family Violence Lab: University of New Hampshire.

Hodgins, S. (1992). Mental disorder, intellectual deficiency, and crime: Evidence from a birth cohort. *Archives of General Psychiatry, 49,* 476-483.

Holtzworth-Munroe, A., Bates, L., Smutzler, N., & Sandin, E. (1997). A brief review of the research on husband violence. *Aggression and Violent Behavior, 1,* 65-99.

Holtzworth-Munroe, A., & Stuart, G. (1994). Typologies of male batterers: Three subtypes and the differences among them. *Psychological Bulletin, 116,* 476-497.

Island, D., & Letellier, P. (1991). *Men who beat the men who love them.* New York: Harrington Park.

Johnson, M. P. (1995). Patriarchal terrorism and common couple violence: Two forms of violence against women. *Journal of Marriage and the Family, 57,* 283-294.

Kropp, P. R., & Hart, S. D. (2000). The Spousal Assault Risk Assessment (SARA) Guide: Reliability and validity. *Law & Human Behavior, 24,* 101-118.

Kwong, M. J., & Bartholomew, K. (1998). *Gender differences in domestic violence in the city of Vancouver.* Paper presented at the annual meeting of the American Psychological Association, San Francisco, CA.

Kwong, M. J., Bartholomew, K., & Dutton, D. G. (1999). Gender differences in patterns of relationship violence in Alberta. *Canadian Journal of Behavioral Science, 31,* 150-160.

Lewis, S. F., Travea, L., & Fremouw, W. J. (2002). Characteristics of female perpetrators and victims of dating violence. *Violence & Victims, 17(5),* 593-606.

Lie, G. Y., & Gentlewarrier, S. (1991). Intimate violence in lesbian relationships: Discussion of survey findings and practice implications. *Journal of Social Service Research, 15,* 41-59.

Lie, G. Y., Schilit, R., Bush, J., Montagne, M., & Reyes, L. (1991). Lesbians in currently aggressive relationships: How frequently do they report aggressive past relationships? *Violence and Victims, 6,* 121-135.

Loucks, A. D., & Zamble, E. (2000). Predictors of criminal behavior and prison misconduct in serious female offenders. *Empirical and Applied Criminal Justice Review, 1,* 1-47.

Magdol, L., Moffitt, T. E., Caspi, A., Newman, D. L., Fagan, J., & Silva, P. A. (1997). Gender differences in partner violence in a birth cohort of 21 year olds: Bridging the gap between clinical and epidemiological approaches. *Journal of Consulting and Clinical Psychology, 65,* 68-78.

Majdan, A. (1998). *Prevalence and personality correlates of women's aggression against male partners.* Unpublished master's thesis. Simon Fraser University, Burnaby, British Columbia, Canada.

Makepeace, J. M. (1986). Gender differences in courtship violence victimization. *Family Relations, 35,* 383-388.

Martin, M. (1997). Double your trouble: Dual arrest in family violence. *Journal of Family Violence, 12(2),* 139-157.

Mason, A., & Blankenship, V. (1987). Power and affiliation motivation, stress and abuse in intimate relationships. *Journal of Personality and Social Psychology, 52,* 203-210.

Moffitt, T., Robins, R., & Caspi, A. (2001). A couples analysis of partner abuse with implications for abuse prevention. *Criminology and Public Policy, 1,* 5-36.

Morse, B. (1995). Beyond the conflict tactics scale: Assessing gender differences in partner violence. *Violence and Victims, 10,* 257-272.

Nicholls, T. L., & Dutton, D. G. (2001). Abuse committed by women against male intimates. *Journal of Couples Therapy, 10*, 41-57.

Nicholls, T. L., Desmarais, S., Spidel, A., & Koch, W. (2005). *"Common couple violence" and "intimate terrorism": A study of Johnson's typologies.* Manuscript in preparation. University of British Columbia, Vancouver, BC, Canada.

Nicholls, T. L., Ogloff, J. R. P., & Douglas, K. S. (2004). Assessing risk for violence among female and male civil psychiatric patients: The HCR-20, PCL:SV, and McNiel & Binder's VSC. *Behavioral Sciences and the Law, 22*, 127-158.

O'Keefe, N. K., Brockopp, K., & Chew, E. (1986). Teen dating violence. *Social Work, 31*, 465-468.

Renzetti, C. M. (1992). *Violent betrayal: Partner abuse in lesbian relationships.* Thousand Oaks, CA.

Ridley, C. A., & Feldman, C. M. (2003). Female domestic violence toward male partners: Exploring conflict responses and outcomes. *Journal of Family Violence, 18(3)*, 157-170.

Rosenfeld, B. (1992). Court-ordered treatment of spouse abuse. *Clinical Psychology Review, 12*, 205-226.

Saunders, D. G. (1986). When battered women use violence: Husband abuse or self defense. *Violence and Victims, 1*, 47-60.

Saunders, D. (1988). Wife abuse, husband abuse or mutual combat: A feminist perspective on the empirical findings. In Yllo, K. & Bograd, M. (Eds.), *Feminist perspectives on wife assault* (pp. 90-113). Newbury Park: Sage.

Simonelli, C. J., & Ingram, K. M., (1998). Psychological distress among men experiencing physical and emotional abuse in heterosexual dating relationships. *Journal of Interpersonal Violence, 13*, 667-681.

Sommer, R., Barnes, G. E., & Murray, R. P. (1992), Alcohol consumption, alcohol abuse, personality and female perpetrated spouse abuse. *Personality and Individual Differences, 13(12)*, 1315-1323.

Sorenson, S. B., Upchurch, D. M., & Shen, H. (1996). Violence and injury in marital arguments: Risk patterns and gender differences. *American Journal of Public Health, 66(1)*, 35-40.

Spidel, A., Nicholls, T. L., Kendrick, K., Klein, C., & Kropp, R. P. (2004, March). *Characteristics of female intimate partner assaulters.* Paper presented at the annual meeting of the American Psychology-Law Society, Scottsdale, AZ.

Spidel, A., Nicholls, T., & Kropp, R. P. (2003, April). *Personality and demographic characteristics of female who abuse their male partners.* Paper presented at the annual meeting of the International Association of Forensic Mental Health Services, Miami, FL.

Steinmetz, S. K. (1977-78). The battered husband syndrome. *Victimology: An International Journal, 2*, 499-509.

Stets, J. E., & Pirog-Good, M. A. (1987). Violence in dating relationships. *Social Psychology Quarterly, 50*, 237-246.

Stets, J., & Straus, M. A. (1990). Gender differences in reporting marital violence and its medical and psychological consequences. In M. Straus & R. Gelles (Eds.), *Physical violence in American families: Risk factors and adaptations to violence in 8,145 families* (pp. 227-244). New Brunswick, NJ: Transaction.

Straus, M. A. (1979). Measuring intrafamily conflict and violence: The Conflict Tactics (CT) scales. *Journal of Marriage and the Family, 41*, 75-88.

Straus, M. A. (1990). Measuring intrafamily conflict and violence: The Conflict Tactics (CT) Scales. In M. A. Straus & R. J. Gelles (Eds.), *Physical violence in American families: Risk factors and adaptations to violence in 8,145 families* (pp. 29-47). New Brunswick, NJ: Transaction.

Straus, M. A. (1999). The controversy over domestic violence by women: A methodological, theoretical, and sociology of science analysis. In X. B. Arriaga & S. Oskamp (Eds.), *Violence in intimate relationships* (pp. 17-44). Thousand Oaks, CA: Sage.

Straus, M. A., & Gelles, R. J. (1992). How violent are American families? Estimates from the National Family Violence Resurvey and other studies. In M. A. Straus & R. J. Gelles (Eds.), *Physical violence in the American family* (pp. 95-112). Transaction Publishers: New Brunswick, New Jersey.

Straus, M. A., Hamby, S. L., Boney-McCoy, S., & Sugarman, D. B. (1996). The revised Conflict Tactics Scale (CTS2). *Journal of Family Issues, 17*, 283-316.

Thompson, E. H. (1991). The maleness of violence in dating relationships: An appraisal of stereotypes. *Sex Roles, 24*, 261-278.

Walker, L. (1984). *The battered woman syndrome.* New York: Springer.

Werner, N. E., & Crick, N. R. (1999). Relational aggression and social-psychological adjustment in a college sample. *Journal of Abnormal Psychology, 108*, 615-623.

White, J. W., Smith, P. H., Koss, M. P., & Figueredo, A. J. (2000). Intimate partner aggression–What have we learned? Comment on Archer (2000). *Psychological Bulletin, 126*, 690-696.

AUTHORS' NOTES

Donald G. Dutton, PhD, has published over one hundred papers and three books, including the *Domestic Assault of Women*, *The Batterer*, and *The Abusive Personality: A Psychological Profile*. Dutton has served as an expert witness in criminal trials involving family violence, including his work for the prosecution in the O. J. Simpson trial. He is currently Professor of Psychology at the University of British Columbia (UBC).

Tonia L. Nicholls, PhD, recently completed a Post Doctoral Fellowship with the Department of Psychiatry at UBC. She is a Senior Research Fellow with the BC Forensic Psychiatric Services Commission. She has published on abuse in intimate relationships, violence risk assessment, psychopathy, and the provision of mental health services to pretrial inmates. In 2004, Nicholls received the President's New Researcher Award from the Canadian Psychological Association and the American Psychological Association/APAGS Award for Distinguished Professional Contributions by a Graduate Student.

Alicia Spidel is a PhD candidate in the department of psychology at UBC. She recently received the Michael Smith Foundation for Health Research and the Vancouver Foundation Doctoral Award. She was nominated for the Chris Hatcher Memorial Scholarship in 2004 and holds research grants from APLS, APA, AAFP. Her research interests include spousal assault, psychopathy, deception, personality disorders, and mental disordered offenders.

Address correspondence to Dr. Don Dutton, Department of Psychology, University of British Columbia, 2513 West Mall, Vancouver, BC, Canada, V6T 1Y7 (E-mail: dondutton@shaw.ca).

Women Who Perpetrate Relationship Violence: Moving Beyond Political Correctness. Pp. 33-61.
Available online at http://www.haworthpress.com/web/JOR
doi:10.1300/J076v41n04_02

Exploring the Relevance of Attachment Theory as a Dependent Variable in the Treatment of Women Mandated into Treatment for Domestic Violence Offenses

MICHELLE MOHR CARNEY
FREDERICK P. BUTTELL

ABSTRACT *Objective:* The purpose of the study was to: (a) investigate the pre-treatment levels of interpersonal dependency and violence among women entering a 16-week, court-mandated, batterer intervention program (BIP) and determine if there were any associations between interpersonal dependency and violence; (b) investigate differences in demographic variables and psychological variables between treatment completers and drop-outs; and (c) evaluate the treatment effect of a standard BIP in altering levels of interpersonal dependency among treatment completers.

Method: The study employed a secondary analysis of 75 women, 39 treatment completers and 36 drop-outs.

Results: Analysis indicated that women who assault their intimate partners and are court-ordered into treatment are excessively dependent on their partners prior to beginning treatment, that level of interpersonal dependency is directly related to a multidimensional conceptualization of domestic violence (i.e., psychological aggression, physical assault, sexual coercion and injury), that interpersonal dependency is an important variable in predicting treatment completion and that the BIP increased the level of interpersonal dependency among treatment completers.

Conclusion: Implications of the findings for professionals providing intervention services to women in court-mandated batterer intervention programs were explored and discussed. *[Article copies available for a fee from The Haworth Document Delivery Service: 1-800-HAWORTH. E-mail address: <docdelivery@haworthpress.com> Website: <http://www.HaworthPress.com>* © 2005 by The Haworth Press, Inc. All rights reserved.]

KEYWORDS Attachment theory, women offenders, batterer intervention programs

Although the prevalence and consequences of male violence directed towards women in intimate relationships has been well established [for a recent review, see Lawson, (2003)], the research on violent women in intimate relationships is far less developed. The primary reason for this situation is the highly charged and frequently acrimonious debate about whether "husband battering" actually exists (Pagelow, 1992). The crux of the debate hinges on the data generated from two, mutually exclusive, data sets. Data from nationally representative surveys suggest that men and women are equally violent in intimate relationships (Straus, 1999), a conclusion borne out by Archer's (2000, 2002) meta-analysis of 82 couple-conflict studies which found that women were more likely to use physical aggression than men and to resort to violence more often than men. This data is directly contrasted by data generated from the Bureau of Justice Statistics (BJS) that has consistently indicated that women are five times more likely than men to have been the victims of domestic violence (Rennison & Welchans, 2000). These different data sets have led to diametrically opposed conceptualizations of domestic violence. On one side are those aligned with the national family violence surveys who believe that women are as violent as men in intimate relationships (e.g., McNeely, Cook & Torres, 2001), while, on the other side, are those who believe men are the primary aggressors in intimate relationships. Opponents of the latter position purport that the survey data fails to account for either the context in which domestic violence takes place or the differential consequences of violence for men and women (e.g., Kimmel, 2002). Recently, the debate has taken on added significance as women are increasingly being arrested for domestic violence offenses and mandated into batterer intervention programs (BIPs) as part of a criminal sentence.

The presence of women, as offenders, in treatment programs for domestic violence offenders, is the direct result of legislation mandating the arrest of perpetrators in cases where police respond to a call and determine that domestic violence has occurred. In brief, in the late 1980s, most states enacted Law Enforcement Protection legislation. This legislation, commonly referred to as "warrantless arrest," allows police who respond to a domestic violence call to arrest the abuser and press charges themselves. In these cases, the victim does not have to file a warrant against the abuser before an arrest is made. These laws remove the burden of pressing charges from the victim and have resulted in a substantial increase in the number of domestic violence arrests and convictions. Interestingly, this same legislation has resulted in a significant number of women being arrested and prosecuted for domestic violence offenses (Martin, 1997). Although the arrest of women was clearly an unintended consequence of mandatory arrest statutes (Swan & Snow, 2002), their sudden appearance in court-mandated treatment programs has had a dramatic impact on the national debate regarding female initiated violence. As a result of women being court-mandated into batterer treatment programs, it is no longer possible to suggest that women are infrequently the initiators of violence in their intimate relationships (Carlsten, 2002). If this were true, there would be very few women arrested, successfully prosecuted, and mandated into treatment as part of a criminal sentence. Unfortunately, however, there is very little empirical information available about female domestic violence offenders and, currently, women convicted of domestic violence offenses are mandated into BIPs designed to intervene with male offenders (Dowd, 2001).

SIMILARITIES BETWEEN WOMEN AND MEN WHO PERPETRATE VIOLENCE

Given the politics surrounding the issue of female violence occurring in intimate relationships, it is not surprising that much of the available research on this topic has been devoted to fleshing out differences between men and women arrested for domestic violence offenses (Fiebert & Gonzalez, 1997; Hamberger, 1997; Hamberger, Lohr, & Bonge, 1994; Hamberger & Potente, 1994; Martin, 1997; Miller, 2001; Morse, 1995; Swan & Snow, 2002). The effect of this small body of research has been to delineate differential causes and consequences of intimate partner violence for both male and female participants.

More recently, the issue of how men and women in BIPs may be similar has been addressed in several studies, the findings of which suggest that women may be more similar to men than was previously expected. For example, in a recent study of 52 women referred to treatment for abusive behaviors, women who were violent towards their partner only (PO) were found to use controlling violence less frequently, defensive or reactive violence more frequently, report witnessing their mothers' physical violence less frequently and report fewer traumatic symptoms, relative to women who were generally violent (GV) (Babcock, Miller & Saird, 2003). In this respect, women in BIPs may be similar to men in BIPs in that there might be within group differences along several dimensions, which might hold promise for different clinical interventions [for a recent review of male, batterer subtypes, see Holtzworth et al. (2000)]. Other recent studies have suggested that women and men referred to BIPs are more similar than dissimilar. Specifically, Busch and Rosenberg (2004) discovered that women were similar to men in terms of their use of severe violence, inflicting severe injuries on their partners, use of violence against non-intimates and usage of alcohol and/or drugs at the time of their arrest. Similarly, Henning, Jones and Holdford (2003) discovered that the women were demographically similar to the men in terms of childhood experiences, exposure to interparental conflict and mental health history.

The Role of Attachment Theory

Given the similarities between women and men in treatment for domestic violence offenses, the recent experimental evaluations of BIP effectiveness for male batterers, which have suggested that they are having either little or no treatment effect (Dunford, 2000; Feder & Forde, 2000; Davis & Taylor, 1999; Davis, Taylor & Maxwell, 1998), may have implications for female offenders as well. In brief, as the research suggesting that BIPs are having small treatment effects has accumulated, some authors have advocated for expanding our conceptualization of theories regarding what causes domestic violence (Lawson, 2003; Rosenbaum & Leisring, 2003). According to Sonkin and Dutton (2003), the most promising of these theories is attachment theory. Interestingly, the focus on attachment theory was the direct result of observations made in clinical practice that male batterers were overly dependent on their intimate partners but incapable of initiating and maintaining an emotionally supportive relationship. As a result, these men desired closeness with their partners but, given their inability to achieve emotional closeness, engaged in violent and controlling behaviors to ensure physical closeness rather than emotional closeness (Murphy et al., 1994).

Evaluating the quality of childhood attachment patterns in adult samples is extremely difficult. Researchers often use indirect measures, most commonly interpersonal dependency, to judge the quality of childhood attachment in adults. Conceptually, excessive interpersonal dependency among abusive men is viewed as a consequence of insecure attachment in childhood (Dutton, 1995, 2000; Holtzworth-Monroe et al., 1997). In brief, attachment theory proposes that the overall quality of the infant-caretaker relationship during infancy and early childhood is both the primary determinant of dependent traits in adulthood (Ainsworth, 1969) and a model for later interpersonal relationships (Bowlby, 1980). Regarding the development of excessive interpersonal dependency among batterers, Dutton (1995) has argued that battered mothers cannot adequately attend to the demands of the attachment process while simultaneously attempting to negotiate a hostile and dangerous home environment. Consequently, children in this situation become insecurely attached and, in adulthood, exhibit excessive dependency on their partners (Dutton, 1995, 2000; Holtzworth-Monroe et al., 1997; Murphy et al., 1994). Recently, Sonkin and Dutton (2003) have reviewed the literature on attachment theory and domestically violent men and suggest that "men whose violence was predominantly or exclusively in intimate relationships probably have an attachment disorder" (p. 109). Therefore, they conclude, "incorporating attachment theory into batterer treatment is well founded" (p. 110). Despite the apparent connection between attachment theory and male batterers, there have been no studies exploring the relevance of attachment theory to female batterers. According to Henning, Jones and Holdford (2003), such a study would be of critical importance because "exploring the attachment styles of female offenders and their attitudes towards the use of physical aggression will be helpful in determining whether these theories can account for female-perpetrated intimate partner abuse" (p. 851).

Given the absence of information on the role of attachment theory in explaining the development of violence among female batterers, the purpose of the present research was to investigate the following three research questions: (1) What are the pre-treatment levels of interpersonal dependency and violence among women entering a 16-week, court-mandated BIP and are there any associations between interpersonal dependency and violence? (2) Are there differences in demographic variables and psychological variables between treatment completers and drop-outs? and (3) What is the effect of a standard BIP in altering levels of interpersonal dependency among treatment completers?

METHOD

Data Collection

This study employed a secondary analysis of data collected by the Bay Oaks Professional Associates, a non-profit agency in Mobile, Alabama, that has been providing counseling services to court-mandated clients since 1993. At the intake interview, clients are required to complete a demographic questionnaire and two psychological instruments [i.e., the Revised Conflict Tactics Scales (CTS2) (Straus, Hamby, Boney-McCoy & Sugarman, 1996; and the Interpersonal Dependency Inventory (IDI) (Hirschfield et al., 1977)]. On the final day of the batterer intervention program, clients are required to complete the IDI. The agency uses this information to create a pre-treatment assessment of the individual and to evaluate changes in interpersonal dependency. In order to protect the privacy of the women in the study, the researchers were not given direct access to client files. Rather, an employee of the agency gained consent from the participating women and deleted personal information from the demographic information form (e.g., name, address, place of employment), copied both this form and the psychological instruments, and provided the researchers with this modified data. In using these procedures, the researchers were able to generate the information needed to conduct the research, while maintaining the privacy of the women in the treatment program.

Operational Definitions of "Treatment Completer" and "Drop-Out"

Given the high rates of attrition associated with BIPs serving male batterers [national attrition averages 50% (Gondolf, 1997)], many researchers have adopted a definition for "completer" that would be more accurately described as "partial completer" (Daly, Power & Gondolf, 2001; Pirog-Good & Stets-Kealey, 1986; Rosenfeld, 1992). Specifically, because so many men fail to fully complete the batterer intervention program, researchers have conceptualized men as "completers" if they completed some fraction of the prescribed treatment (e.g., four weeks of a 12-week program). The problem with such a definition is that it equates men who complete a portion of the program with men who complete the entire program. Certainly, there are differences between these two groups and the men who complete the entire program are likely to benefit more than men who complete a fraction of it (Hamberger & Hastings, 1988). If this is not the case, why have a treatment program that is 16 weeks long instead of one that is four weeks long? Clearly, the premise is that all of the material in the program is important for modifying behavior and, therefore, an accurate definition of "completer" should entail finishing the entire program. Consequently, extrapolating from the literature on male batterers, this study defined "treatment completers" as those women who successfully finished the 16-week treatment program and "drop-outs" as those women who failed to successfully finish the program.

Participants

The agency has been using the combination of assessment tools described above since August 1999. Since that time, 152 women have been referred to the 16-week program by the courts. Of this group of women, 77 women (51%) have dropped out of the program, 41 women (25%) have graduated from the program and 36 women (24%) are still active in the program. The sample for this study included all 16-week treatment completers (n = 41) and a random sample of 40 dropouts. Of the 81 women originally selected for the sample, six were omitted from the analysis because they repeatedly gave the same rating to all the items and were clearly not discriminating among them or they failed to complete the entire instrument package. Thus, the final sample of batterers consisted of 75 participants, 39 treatment completers and 36 dropouts. Within this sample of court-mandated referrals, 34% were referred following an arrest for severe physical violence, 25% for moderate physical violence, and 41% for mild physical violence, with treatment completers significantly more often referred following mild physical violence ($\chi^2 = 13.700$, $p = .001$) than dropouts.

Most participants were not married (68%), averaged 29 years of age, with a twelfth grade education. The sample included African-American (72.0%) and Caucasian (28.0%) women averaging one previous arrest for domestic violence. Table 1 shows the general characteristics of the sample at the pre-treatment assessment.

In an effort to better understand the levels of interpersonal dependency of the battering sample relative to nonviolent women, a small sample of 25 women with no identified history of domestic violence was recruited from the community to serve as a nonviolent comparison group. Participants were adult women, recruited through flyers, who were asked to complete the measure of interpersonal dependency. This sample of community women was chosen to provide normative information regarding nonviolent women's levels of interpersonal dependency. Though they are likely different from the women comprising the experimental group in terms of education and socioeconomic status, they provide a practical comparison group for enhancing our understanding of interpersonal dependency among adult women and, by extension, the quality of childhood attachment patterns in adult women. It is important to note, however, that all the women came from the same community in the same region of the country and, therefore, share experiences relative to that geographic region.

☐ **Table 1: Participant Characteristics**

Characteristic	Treatment Completers (n = 39)	Drop-outs (n = 36)	Total (n = 75)
	M (SD)	M (SD)	M (SD)
1. Age	31.0 (8.4)	27.5 (7.8)	29.3 (8.3)
2. Prior Arrests	1.1 (1.7)	1.9 (1.5)	1.4 (1.7)
3. Prior Arrests D.V.**	.6 (.7)	1.7 (1.3)	.9 (1.0)
4. Education*	12.4 (1.8)	11.6 (1.1)	12.0 (1.6)
5. IDI pretreatment*	52.3 (6.7)	55.8 (8.6)	54.0 (7.0)
	n (%)	n (%)	n (%)
Race: 1. African-American 2. Caucasian	 30 (76.9) 9 (23.1)	 24 (66.7) 12 (33.3)	 54 (72.0) 21 (28.0)
Offense at Referral*** 1. Mild Physical Violence 2. Moderate Physical Violence 3. Severe Physical Violence	 21 (53.8) 3 (7.7) 15 (38.5)	 10 (27.8) 16 (44.4) 10 (27.8)	 31 (41.4) 19 (25.3) 25 (33.3)
Status of Relationship* 1. Married 2. Not Married	 12 (30.8) 27 (69.2)	 24 (66.7) 12 (33.3)	 51 (68.0) 24 (32.0)

Note: * $p < .05$; ** $p < .005$; *** $p < .001$

The Batterer Intervention Program

The site for this study was a non-profit organization that has been providing counseling services to the Mobile, Alabama, community for the past 10 years. Since 1993, this agency has been treating convicted domestic violence offenders. The program is part of a collaborative effort (involving the police, the court, and agency staff) aimed at intervening in violent relationships to reduce the occurrence of domestic violence in the community. The creation of the batterer intervention program was a response to the passage of the Alabama Law Enforcement Protection Act of 1989 discussed previously. Because of the passing of the Law Enforcement Protection Act, the police have engaged in a proarrest policy, the courts have mandated counseling for the batterer as part of the sentence, and as mentioned previously, BIPs were developed to provide intervention services to male batterers. Consequently, women convicted of domestic violence offenses are being treated in BIPs designed for male offenders (Dowd, 2001).

The intervention program evaluated in this study is cognitive-behavioral in orientation and is consistent in organization and focus to those programs described in the literature (Gondolf, 1997; Rosenbaum & Leisring, 2001; Williams, 1992). The intervention program is a structured, intensive, 16-week, group treatment program that focuses primarily on anger management and skills development. The intervention program incorporates two phases: (a) orientation and intake interview (one session); and (b) psychoeducational classes (15 sessions). Groups consist of approximately 15 batterers and meet one night each week for approximately two hours. This batterer treatment program incorporates confrontation, therapy, and educational components. In this setting, the common proximal events of domestic violence are directly addressed with clients and they are given an opportunity to make changes that will positively affect their personal relationships with others.

The 15-week psychoeducational program curriculum can be broken up into three successive series of group experiences. Because most offenders share a common set of defenses (minimization, denial, and blame) that foster aggressive behavior, the first series of group sessions helps participants to recognize and overcome these defense mechanisms. In this series, participants are assisted in overcoming their natural resistance to change by helping them achieve insight into their use of defense mechanisms. Thus, the first step toward modifying behavior occurs when clients recognize and accept the fact that the problem is their behavior. The second series of sessions flows out of the fact that the belief and value systems of most batterers are very similar and foster the notion of traditional sex roles stereotypes. This series challenges the batterers' beliefs and values. The sessions are designed to help clients restructure their thinking by modifying the beliefs that promote violent behavior. The final series of sessions is designed to help clients increase interpersonal skills by providing them with a repertoire of alternate and appropriate behaviors. In this series, skills such as problem solving, assertiveness, and negotiation are both taught and practiced in the group setting. Typically, in the psychoeducational series, the first series lasts 4 weeks and the second and third series are approximately 4 weeks and 7 weeks in length, respectively.

Instruments

The Interpersonal Dependency Inventory

The Interpersonal Dependency Inventory (IDI) is a 48-item, self-report instrument designed to measure interpersonal dependency. The authors of the IDI have defined interpersonal dependency as "a complex of thoughts, beliefs, feelings, and behaviors which revolve around the need to associate closely with, interact with, and rely upon valued other people" (Hirschfield et al., 1977, p. 610). The authors identify three conceptual sources for the concept of interpersonal dependency that include (a) the psychoanalytic theory of object relations, (b) social learning theories of dependency, and (c) the ethological theory of attachment (Hirschfield et al., 1977). According to Hirschfield et al. (1977), dependency results from the quality of the infant-caretaker relationship (i.e., psychoanalytic theory of object relations), learned behaviors (i.e., social learning theory) and the interaction between them (i.e., ethological theory). As mentioned previously, evaluating the quality of childhood attachment patterns in adult samples is extremely difficult and researchers often use indirect measures, most commonly interpersonal dependency, to judge the quality of childhood attachment in adults.

Respondents were asked to read each of the 48 items and to rate each of the items on a 4-point scale ranging from 1 *not characteristic of me* to 4 *very characteristic of me*. Examples of some of the items respondents were asked to rate are "I prefer to be by myself" and "It is hard for me to ask someone for a favor." Three subscales were derived from the instrument: (a) emotional reliance on another person (ER), (b) lack of social self-confidence (LS), and (c) assertion of autonomy (AA). This study utilized a revised scoring procedure recommended by one of the original developers of the IDI that "maximizes the identification of interpersonal dependency" (Gough, personal communication, September 26, 1996). This scoring strategy contends that elevated scores on the LS subscale result in a higher score on the AA subscale (i.e., the AA score elevates as an ego defense against the feelings expressed in the LS subscale). In order to incorporate this view into the scoring strategy, a fourth score is computed, which is the product of the scores on LS and AA divided by 30. The product of LS and AA is divided by 30 to keep the magnitude of the score on the fourth variable similar to the others. The four variables are then combined in the following equation: interpersonal dependency = 40.84 + .20 (ER) + .18 (LS) − .66 (AA) + .53 (LS × AA/30). In this equation, the constant of 40.84 is used to produce means approximating 50 on large, heterogeneous samples and, in such samples, standard deviations of 6 can be expected (Gough, personal communication, September 26, 1996). Thus, in this scoring procedure, a total score of 56 would signify strong feelings of dependency while a total score of 44 would signify feelings of independence and self-sufficiency. Although, currently, there is no normative data available on this revised scoring system, the present study employed this scoring system in computing IDI total scores. Importantly, this scoring equation was also employed by Buttell and Jones (2001), in a study investigating interpersonal dependency among male batterers court-mandated into treatment for domestic violence offenses.

According to Bornstein (1994), the IDI is one of the most widely used dependency scales and it has been used in more than 25 empirical studies since it was first published in 1977. Perhaps most importantly, it is the most widely used instrument to evaluate interpersonal dependency, and thereby childhood attachment patterns, among studies involving batterers. Hirschfield et al. (1977) indicated that the IDI has good internal consistency (e.g., split-half reliabilities for the three subscales ranging from .72 to .91) and good concurrent validity with the subscales for emotional reliance and lack of social self-confidence correlating significantly with measures of general neuroticism (e.g., Maudley Personality Inventory) and anxiety, depression, and interpersonal sensitivity (e.g., Symptom Checklist-90). Scores on the IDI subscales are unrelated to age, years of education, marital status, social desirability, or socioeconomic status (Hirschfield et al., 1977; Bornstein, 1994). Bornstein (1994) has reviewed the last 15 years of empirical research involving the IDI and concludes that there is ample evidence to support the construct validity of the scale as a measure of interpersonal dependency. Additionally, there is evidence from research involving university students and psychiatric patients, indicating that the IDI can distinguish between psychiatric patients and normals (Hirschfield et al., 1977).

The Revised Conflict Tactics Scales

The Revised Conflict Tactics Scales (CTS2) (Straus, Hamby, Boney-McCoy & Sugarman, 1996) is an enhanced version of the original Conflict Tactics Scales (CTS) (Straus, 1979, 1997), which is a widely accepted self-report measure of physical assaults in domestic relationships. In fact, the CTS is the most widely used self-report measure of domestic violence in the U.S. (Dwyer, 1999; Straus, 1997). The revised scale has enhanced content validity and reliability, with two additional scales measuring sexual coercion and physical injury, and better differentiation between minor and severe levels within each of the five scales. The resulting CTS2 is a comprehensive 39-item, self-report instrument designed to measure negotiation skills, psychological and physical attacks, use of sexual coercion, and physical injury on a partner in a marital, cohabiting, or dating relationship over the previous 12 months (Straus, Hamby, Boney-McCoy & Sugarman, 1996; Straus, 1997).

The theoretical basis for the CTS2 remains the same as it was in the CTS, conflict theory (Straus, 1979; Straus, Hamby, Boney-McCoy & Sugarman, 1996), which assumes conflict to be a part of human interactions, but does not presume violence to be the reasonable approach to dealing with conflict (Straus, Hamby, Boney-McCoy & Sugarman, 1996; Straus, 1997). The CTS2 measures specific acts of physical violence, not attitudes about or consequences of using violence to deal with conflict (Straus, Hamby, Boney-McCoy & Sugarman, 1996). Additionally, the CTS2 measures the behavior of both partners in the relationship. The instrument is designed in a way that questions first the program participant about their behavior ("I insulted or swore at my partner"), and then about the behavior of their partner ("My partner did this to me") (Straus, Hamby, Boney-McCoy & Sugarman, 1996).

The variables mentioned above are measured on five subscales: (1) negotiation ["actions taken to settle disagreement through discussion" (p. 289)], (2) psychological aggression [acts of aggression that are not physical (i.e., yelling or swearing at partner, stomping out of the room)], (3) physical assault, (4) sexual coercion ["behavior that is intended to compel the partner to engage in unwanted sexual activity . . . from verbal insistence to physical force" (p. 290)], and (5) injury ["partner-inflicted physical injury, as indicated by bone or tissue damage, a need for medical attention, or pain continuing for a day or more" (p. 290)] (Straus, Hamby, Boney-McCoy & Sugarman, 1996). Respondents rate each of the items on a 7-point Likert-style frequency scale (0 = "this has never happened before," 1 = "once in the past year," 2 = "twice in the past year," 3 = "3-5 times in the past year," 4 = "6-10 times in the past year," 5 = "11-20 times in the past year," 6 = "more than 20 times in the past year," and 7 = "not in the past year, but it did happen before"(Straus, Hamby, Boney-McCoy & Sugarman, 1996, p. 311). To create interpretable scores, values 1 and 2 remained the same, and values 3 through 6 were recoded to be the midpoints (3 = 4, 4 = 8, 5 = 15, 6 = 25) (Straus, Hamby, Boney-McCoy & Sugarman, 1996).

The CTS2 can be scored to determine prevalence, chronicity, and frequency of the five scales. Annual prevalence is the most frequently utilized type of score, and indicates whether the respondent reported engaging in any act described within the scale during the previous year. Utilizing the recoded values, the chronicity score represents how often the respondent engaged in the acts described within each scale (for those who engaged in at least one act). To obtain the chronicity scores, the value 7 (not in the past year, but it did happen before) and the value 0 (this has never happened before) are recoded to reflect missing data. The scales are then summed to create a new score indicating chronicity of the acts in the scales for those who experienced at least one event. Similarly, the frequency score is obtained by summing the values within the scales, however, zero values (0 and 7) are not recoded as missing data but reflected in the total to represent the infrequency of the behaviors for various participants in the study.

In addition to prevalence, chronicity, and frequency, severity of physical assaults is an important factor. The authors of the CTS2 suggest that two subscales be created to account for minor (i.e., slapping or shoving) and severe (i.e., using a weapon) levels of assault (Straus, Hamby, Boney-McCoy & Sugarman, 1996). For this study, annual prevalence and annual chronicity scores were computed for each of the five scales of the CTS2. Furthermore, each of the five subscales (negotiation, psychological aggression, physical assault, sexual coercion and injury) were divided by level of severity (minor vs. severe) and re-scored for use in the analysis.

The CTS has been used with individuals from varying races, cultures and ethnic background, including the African-American group represented in this study (Cazenave & Straus, 1979; DuRant, Cadenhead, Pendergrast, Slavens & Linder, 1994; Hampton, Gelles & Harrop, 1989). Additionally, the reliability and validity of the CTS has been well established in previous studies (for examples, see Straus & Gelles, 1990; Straus, 1997). The authors of the CTS2 report reliability ranging from .79 to .95, and provide preliminary evidence of construct validity and discriminant validity (Straus, Hamby, Boney-McCoy & Sugarman, 1996; Straus, 1997).

RESULTS

Question 1: What are the pre-treatment levels of interpersonal dependency and violence among women entering a 16-week, court-mandated BIP and are there any associations between interpersonal dependency and violence?

Table 1 shows the general characteristics of the sample at the pre-treatment assessment. Given this study's reliance on a revised scoring procedure for the IDI and, in order to get a better understanding of the pre-treatment level of interpersonal dependency among this sample of court-mandated batterers, the total sample of batterers was compared to a group of 25 women drawn from the community, all of whom had no identified history of domestic violence. With an alpha level of .05, an independent t-test procedure indicated that there was a significant difference (t (99) = 3.02, $p < .01$) between the batterers and the nonviolent comparison group on the pre-treatment level of interpersonal dependency. The total sample of batterers scored significantly higher on the IDI (M = 54.0, SD = 7.0) than the nonviolent comparison group (M = 50.1, SD = 5.3) at the pre-treatment assessment.

The CTS2 was utilized to measure program par icipants on individual and partner conflict tactics. Scores on the each of the five subscales of the CTS2 were examined for prevalence and chronicity, overall, as well as separated by minor and severe levels of behaviors. The prevalence of each act in the subscales 12 months prior to program entry reveals only the presence of the behavior. Both program completers and dropouts reported using negotiation tactics with their partners (96.0%; completers = 92.3%, drop-outs = 100.0%), as well as psychologically aggressive tactics with their partners (90.7%; completers = 84.6%, drop-outs = 92.7%). Participants also reported using physical violence, both minor (81.3%; completers = 69.2%, drop-outs = 94.4%) and severe (45.3%; completers = 38.5%, drop-outs = 52.8%), and minor sexual coercion (18.7%; completers = 7.7%, drop-outs = 30.6%). Only dropouts reported using severe sexual coercion (8.0%). Both completers and dropouts reported using violence resulting in sustained injuries at both the minor (53.3%; completers = 46.2%, drop-outs = 61.1%) and severe (16.0%; completers = 7.7%, drop-outs = 25.0%) levels.

The chronicity score represents how often (number of times) the respondent engaged in the acts within each scale (for those who engaged in at least one act). CTS2 subscale scores for negotiation, verbal aggression, physical assault, sexual coercion and injury are summarized in Table 2. Both program completers and dropouts reported using negotiation tactics with their partners an average of 68 times in the year preceding treatment (completers–M = 35.3, SD = 5.9, drop-outs–M = 44.2, SD = 7.4), as well as psychologically aggressive tactics with their partners an average of 39 times in the preceding year (completers–M = 14.9, SD = 2.6, drop-outs = M = 37.1, SD = 6.3). Participants also reported chronically using minor physical violence an average of 18 times (completers–M = 13.1, SD = 12.8, drop-outs–M = 22.5, SD = 29.7) and severe physical violence an average of 14 times in the year preceding treatment (completers–M = 4.6, SD = 3.3, drop-outs–M = 21.1, SD = 37.0). Dropouts reported both minor and severe chronic sexual coercion (minor–M = 18.1, SD = 10.2, severe–M = 18.0, SD = 7.7), while completers reported only minor chronic sexual coercion (M = 2.0, SD = 0.0). Both completers and dropouts reported chronically using violence resulting in minor and severe sustained injuries an average of 7 times (minor: completers–M = 3.3, SD = 3.2, drop-outs–M = 10.2, SD = 9.8; severe: completers–M = 2.0, SD = 0.0, drop-outs–M = 8.1, SD = 12.4) in the year preceding treatment. Program dropouts were significantly more likely to chronically use psychologically aggressive tactics ($t = -4.520, p = .000$), minor sexual coercion ($t = -5.251, p = .000$), and violence resulting in minor sustained injuries ($t = -1.474, p = .004$) in the twelve months prior to program entry than program completers.

To gain a better understanding of the findings presented in Table 2, it is important to reiterate the difference between prevalence and chronicity. Prevalence refers only to presence of the behavior in the last year, the participants either used the tactic or they did not. Chronicity refers to how chronic was the use of the tactic for those who engaged in the behavior at least once in the year preceding treatment. An examination of Table 2 indicates seemingly large differences between completers and dropouts on tactic prevalence and chronicity that would seem to be statistically significant, yet they are not. For example, the prevalence of psychologically aggressive tactic use among completers and dropouts was not significantly different (84.6% versus 97.2%), yet when participants did engage in psychologically aggressive tactics, dropouts were

☐ **Table 2: Participant's Prevalence and Chronicity Statistics on the CTS2**

Scale	Completers (n = 39)	Drop-outs (n = 36)
PREVALENCE (use or no use)	% (n)	% (n)
Negotiation	92.3 (36)	100.0 (36)
Psychological Aggression	84.6 (33)	97.2 (35)
Physical Assault		
−minor**	69.2 (27)	94.4 (34)
−severe	38.5 (15)	52.8 (19)
Sexual Coercion		
−minor**	7.7 (3)	30.6 (11)
−severe**	0.0 (0)	16.7 (6)
Injury		
−minor	46.2 (18)	61.1 (22)
−severe*	7.7 (3)	25.0 (9)
CHRONICITY (if use, how often)	M (SD)	M (SD)
Negotiation	65.0 (35.3)	71.2 (44.2)
Psychological Aggression***	23.5 (14.9)	54.1 (37.1)
Physical Assault		
−minor	13.1 (12.8)	22.5 (29.7)
−severe	4.6 (3.3)	21.1 (37.0)
Sexual Coercion		
−minor***	2.0 (0.0)	18.1 (10.2)
−severe[a]	0.0	18.0 (7.7)
Injury		
−minor**	3.3 (3.2)	10.2 (9.8)
−severe	2.0 (0.0)	8.1 (12.4)

Note: $*p < .05$, $** p < .01$, $*** p < .001$. *Minor* = Tactic "expressed," "enacted," "perpetrated," "inflicted." *Severe* = Tactic "experienced," "received," "victimized," "sustained." [a] t not computed.

significantly more chronic in their use–an average of 54 times in the previous year compared to 24 times among completers. Conversely, dropouts were significantly more likely to engage in minor physical violence (94.4% versus 69.2%) in the year preceding treatment than were completers, yet their use of the tactics was not significantly more chronic–an average of 23 times in the previous year compared to 13 times among completers.

To determine potential linear relationships between measures of self-reported violence (CTS2) and interpersonal dependency (IDI), a

Pearson product-moment correlation procedure was conducted. Correlations among the CTS2 scale items have been previously established (Straus, Hamby, Boney-McCoy & Sugarman, 1996) and, therefore, the 5 subscale items (negotiation, psychological aggression, physical assault, sexual coercion, and injury) were utilized as a set to investigate the potential correlations between the CTS2 subscales and the IDI at the pretreatment assessment. The subscales of physical assault, sexual coercion, and injury were further divided by level of severity (minor vs. severe) to explore possible associations among these variables and the IDI. Using the Bonferroni approach to control for Type 1 error across the eight correlations, a p value of less than .006 (.05/10) was required for significance (Green, Slakind & Akey, 2000). The results of the correlational analyses presented in Table 3 show that seven of the eight correlations were statistically significant and were greater than or equal to .35, moderate to strong, positive correlations. The correlation between the minor sustained injury subscale score and interpersonal dependency was lower and not significant. In general, the results suggest that self-reported violence (measured by the CTS-2) is positively correlated with interpersonal dependency (measured by the IDI).

Question 2: Are there differences in demographic variables and psychological variables between treatment completers and dropouts?

Table 1 shows the IDI total score and the standard deviation for treatment completers and dropouts at the pre-treatment assessment. With an alpha level of .05, an independent t-test procedure indicated that there was a significant difference ($t = -1.976$, $p = .05$) between the female batterers who completed treatment and those who did not on level of interpersonal dependency. At the pre-treatment assessment dropouts reported higher levels of interpersonal dependency ($M = 55.82$, SD = 8.6) than did completers ($M = 52.25$, SD = 6.7).

Logistic regression was used to analyze the potential impact of demographic, self-reported violence, and interpersonal dependency variables on attrition rates (completion/drop-out) among this sample of 75 women. This study employed an analysis strategy that allowed for simultaneous entry of the independent variables. Table 4 shows the effect of each independent variable on the indicators of treatment completion for the model. It should be noted that the sample for the logistic regression was 72 (96% of the total sample), and satisfies the ratio of 5 cases per variable suggested by Hair et al. (1992).

☐ **Table 3: The Bivariate Correlations Among the CTS2 and the IDI at Pretreatment Assessment**

CTS2	IDI
Negotiation	
Pearson Correlation	.397*
Sig. (2-tailed)	.001
N	72
Psychological Aggression	
Pearson Correlation	.466*
Sig. (2-tailed)	.000
N	72
Physical Assault	
–Minor	
Pearson Correlation	.572*
Sig. (2-tailed)	.000
N	72
–Severe	
Pearson Correlation	.441*
Sig. (2-tailed)	.000
N	72
Sexual Coercion	
–Minor	
Pearson Correlation	.350*
Sig. (2-tailed)	.003
N	72
–Severe	
Pearson Correlation	.498*
Sig. (2-tailed)	.000
N	72
Injury	
–Minor	
Pearson Correlation	.261
Sig. (2-tailed)	.027
N	72
–Severe	
Pearson Correlation	.533*
Sig. (2-tailed)	.000
N	72

Note: *$p < .006$

The overall fit of the model was significant (chi-square = 40.981, df = 7, p = .000). When treatment completion was modeled to be dependent on the seven factors of the model, three of the predictive variables were significant. The frequency of self-reported psychological aggression (Wald χ^2 = 10.875, df = 1, p = .001), physical assault (Wald χ^2 = 6.354, df = 1, p = .012), and sexual coercion (Wald χ^2 = 4.484, df = 1, p = .034) significantly contributed to the prediction of treatment completion among these women.

The coefficients of the logistic regression models are presented in Table 4. The sign of the logistic coefficients (positive or negative) indicate increases or decreases in the dependent variable, with a one-unit change in each independent variable (Hair et al., 1992). For example, the regression coefficient for frequency of psychological aggression was significant, indicating that the use of psychologically aggressive tactics affected the likelihood of treatment completion when the control variables were held constant. For each unit increase in psychological aggression, the odds of treatment completion were increased by a factor of 1.093, when all other independent variables were held constant. Similarly, the odds of treatment completion were increased as the frequency of sexual coercion tactics increased. Conversely, however, the odds of treatment completion decreased as the frequency of physical assault tactics increased.

Predictive Efficacy

Reducing attrition rates for batterer treatment programs may be possible if treatment programs were able to reliably predict treatment completion and non-completion and then focus program efforts to the two groups accordingly. Predictive efficacy, or the objective sought through the use of techniques like logistic regression, refers to the agreement between expected and observed values and is maximized when the expected and observed values are approximate (Visher, Lattimore & Linster, 1991). The observed and predicted instances of program completion were 59.7% (n = 43) for this sample (n = 72, 96% of sample). The percentage of correctly predicted treatment completers (45.8%, n = 33) and correctly predicted treatment dropouts (40.3%, n = 29) resulted in correct classification in 86.1% of the sample. The model incorrectly classified treatment completion in 13.9% (n = 10) of the cases, with 9.7% (n = 7) false positives and 4.2% (n = 3) false negatives. Equally important is the extent to which the model improves, over chance, the identification of treatment completers. To assess the degree to which the measure improved over the chance level of predictive efficacy, the Relative Improvement Over Chance Index (RIOC) was used (see Loeber & Dishion, 1983). Analysis indicated that the model resulted in a 46.1% improvement over chance (50.0% versus 86.1%) in the prediction of treatment completion for the sample.

☐ **Table 4: Logistic Regression Analysis of Treatment Completers and Dropouts**

Variable	Logistic Coefficients		SE	Wald χ^2	Exp(B)
Constant	−1.785		3.356	1.063	.031
IDI Total @ pretreatment	.005		.064	.058	1.016
Negotiation Tactics Frequency	−.008		.010	.893	.991
Psychological Aggression Frequency	.077**		.027	10.875	1.093
Physical Assault Frequency	−.068*		.033	6.354	.920
Sexual Coercion Frequency	.277*		.130	4.484	1.316
Injury Frequency	.074		.093	1.524	1.122
Offense Level @ referral	1.409		.813	3.005	4.091
Log likelihood		58.832			
Model chi-square		40.981**[a]			

Notes: n = 72. [a]$df = 7$. *$p < .05$, ** $p < .001$

Question 3: What is the effect of a standard BIP in altering levels of interpersonal dependency among treatment completers?

Finally, a paired sample *t*-test was conducted to examine the extent to which participants' interpersonal dependency scores changed significantly between the pre-treatment and post-treatment assessments as a result of the BIP. With an alpha level of .05, the dependent *t*-test procedure indicated that scores were significantly different on the IDI post-treatment assessment ($t = -3.729$, p = .001) compared to the pre-treatment assessment. In fact, the mean difference between the pre-treatment ($M = 52.88$, $SD = 6.6$) and the post-treatment ($M = 55.28$, $SD = 6.2$) assessment periods was -2.4 points indicating higher levels of interpersonal dependency upon treatment completion.

DISCUSSION

Question 1: What are the pre-treatment levels of interpersonal dependency and violence among women entering a 16-week, court-mandated BIP and are there any associations between interpersonal dependency and violence?

The results of this study are important because they represent the first empirical investigation of childhood attachment patterns, via levels of interpersonal dependency, among women in treatment for domestic violence offenses. The findings suggest that the women comprising this sample were overly dependent on their partners, an adult indicator of insecure attachment style. Specifically, the data suggests that women court-mandated into a BIP for domestic violence offenses demonstrated elevated levels of interpersonal dependency on their partners, relative to a nonviolent comparison group. In this regard, the findings are important because they suggest that attachment issues, particularly excessive dependency, might become an important target of intervention efforts in BIPs treating female offenders. Perhaps more importantly, if women continue to be treated in intervention programs designed for male offenders, the identification of constructs that have relevance for both male and female batterers is of particular importance.

The data from the CTS2 also provide interesting information about the pervasive nature of violence in the lives of the participants. Although virtually all of the women in the sample (i.e., 96%) indicated that they had attempted to use negotiation skills in resolving conflicts with their partners (i.e., prevalence) and that they did so an average of 68 times in the year preceding the assessment (i.e., chronicity), they also reported high levels of emotional abuse and physical violence. For example, 91% indicated that they had employed psychologically aggressive tactics against their partners, and of those that reported using these tactics, they reported that they used them an average of 39 times in the year preceding treatment. In terms of minor physical violence, 81% of the sample reported engaging in it and doing so an average of 18 times in the year preceding treatment, while 45% of the sample acknowledged using severe physical violence and of doing so an average of 14 times in the year preceding treatment. Finally, 53% of the sample reported using violence that resulted in sustained injuries an average of 7 times annually and approximately 20% of the sample reported that they had employed minor sexual coercion with their partners and that they did so an average of 10 times in the year preceding treatment. Overall, the picture that emerges from this data is one of persistent violence occurring in the lives of these women. The data reviewed above suggests that the women comprising this sample report that they use negotiation weekly, psychological aggression several times a month, both minor and severe physical violence monthly, and violence that results in sustained injury to their intimate partner bi-monthly. Certainly some of these women occupy the dual roles of victim and offender and some unknown percentage were likely using violence in a defensive or retaliatory way. However, setting aside the politically charged debate about whether women are capable of initiating violence in intimate relationships, the sheer level and intensity of violence occurring in these relationships suggests that some sort of intervention should take place. Perhaps the best alternative is to prospectively identify women who are primarily victims or primarily offenders and treat them in separate groups. In this regard, female batterers may be like male batterers in that there might be a differential treatment effect for different "subtypes" of women in BIPs (Saunders, 1996).

The correlational data also provides some interesting information about the relationship between interpersonal dependency and self-reported violence. The findings suggest that the female batterers comprising this sample were overly dependent on their intimate partners and that this excessive level of interpersonal dependency was significantly associated with psychological aggression, physical assault, sexual coercion, and severe injury directed at their intimate partners. In this regard the women comprising this sample appear to be much like male batterers in that there seems to be a positive, linear relationship between interpersonal dependency and a multidimensional definition of violence. If future research confirms this relationship, then attachment theory may become the vehicle to provide gender relevant programming to male and female offenders being treated in the same BIPs.

As mentioned previously, women offenders are currently being treated in BIPs designed for male batterers, which, in the short term, is a situation unlikely to change (Dowd, 2001). Consequently, the identification of treatment constructs that have relevance for both male and female batterers may equip BIPs to modify their existing programming without engaging in wholesale programmatic change or gender specific programming. In the current climate of increasing state standards and legislative requirements for BIPs (Mauiro et al., 2001), wholesale programmatic change would, at best, be unlikely. In terms of interpersonal dependency and attachment theory, the literature on male batterers is evolving in the direction of incorporating these constructs into existing treatment protocols (Sonkin & Dutton, 2003). Consequently, if future research confirms that all batterers, regardless of gender, have dependency issues that should be addressed in BIPs, then dependency and attachment issues may become dependent variables in the treatment of female batterers as well.

Question 2: Are there differences in demographic variables and psychological variables between treatment completers and dropouts?

The findings from this study suggest that drop-outs were more dependent, psychologically aggressive, physically violent and sexually coercive towards their intimate partners than treatment completers. Overall, it appears as if dropouts were significantly more abusive than treatment completers. One interpretation of this finding is that the dropouts in this study were similar to male batterers with dependency issues. For example, the literature on male batterers indicates that men in BIPs are overly dependent on their partners but use physical violence as a substitute for emotional involvement to ensure their partner's ongoing physical closeness. If the dropouts were similar to male batterers in this respect, they may have been driven away from the group by the fact that many of the women in the BIP were both victims and offenders. This key difference may have led them to disrespect their fellow group members for, in their minds, allowing themselves to be abused by their male partners. Consequently, this lack of perceived similarity may have caused them to be dissatisfied with the group members and led to premature termination. Such an explanation is both consistent with our clinical experience in working with women in BIPs and the recent literature identifying within group differences in this population (Babcock, Miller & Saird, 2003).

The results of the logistic regression model have interesting implications for BIPs seeking to improve retention rates for women mandated into BIPs for domestic violence offenses. Regarding male offenders, research into BIP attrition nationally has consistently indicated that approximately 50%-60% of men in BIPs fail to complete treatment (Gondolf, 1997; Lawson, 2003). Many studies have developed significant logistic regression models that accurately predict drop-out among men in the BIPs participating in the study, but studies at different program sites have all created models using different variables. Consequently, there has been no national model that appears to work well for all male batterers attending treatment and the existing literature on this topic frequently reports contradictory findings. For example, some studies have suggested that young, unemployed, men drop out of treatment at greater rates than older men, while other studies have reported the adverse (e.g., Cadsky, Hanson, Crawford & Lalonde, 1996; Hamberger, Lohr & Gottlieb, 2000). Perhaps the best explanation for this confusing situation is that variables like judicial support for a program vary significantly across locations, which serves to confound meaningful synthesis and analysis of attrition in this population [for a review of these issues, see Buttell & Carney (2002)].

The results of this study are important for several reasons. First, they suggest that women drop out of a court-mandated BIP at rates similar to men (i.e., 51%). Second, the findings suggest that interpersonal dependency was an important variable in developing a significant logistic regression model for the women comprising this sample. Perhaps most important is the fact that the model captured 96% of the sample, while correctly classifying 86% of the sample. This represented a 46% improvement over chance. Extrapolating from the literature on attrition among male batterers in BIPs, the findings from this model may only have relevance to the BIP that participated in the study. However, they suggest that robust models can be created in researcher-practitioner partnerships and that interpersonal dependency might be an important variable to consider in creating these models. Additionally, if the BIP is able to use the model to retain even one additional woman that would have otherwise dropped out, it may have important residual effects for the partners and children of these women.

Question 3: What is the effect of a standard BIP in altering levels of interpersonal dependency among treatment completers?

Perhaps the most interesting finding in this study was the discovery that levels of interpersonal dependency were actually higher for treatment completers at the conclusion of the treatment program. This finding is important because it provides initial empirical evidence suggesting that the standard BIP does not decrease the level of interpersonal dependency of female batterers court-mandated into treatment. In fact, it appears as if the adverse may be true. What is particularly troubling was the finding that the sample of female batterers in this study were reporting a level of interpersonal dependency on their partners approximately one standard deviation higher than the nonviolent comparison group and that this level escalates, despite completing treatment. Currently, the impact of this finding on the behaviors of the participants is unknown. However, it is possible that by making these women more dependent on their intimate partners the BIP may, unwittingly, be contributing to these women continuing to abuse their partners. Specifically, if there is a linear relationship between dependency and abuse as some researchers contend (Sonkin & Dutton, 2003), then it seems likely that as dependency escalates, so will abuse. Clearly, however, more research is needed to fully explore the relationship between interpersonal dependency and domestic violence among women in BIPs.

CONCLUSION

When viewed in conjunction with the literature on male batterers and the recent empirical findings suggesting that female batterers might be more like male batterers than was previously expected, it appears that interpersonal dependency and, by extension, attachment patterns may hold considerable potential for helping explain the development of abusive behaviors among women. In brief, the findings from this study suggest that women who assault their male intimate partners and are court-ordered into treatment are excessively dependent on their intimate partners prior to beginning treatment, that level of interpersonal dependency is directly related to a multidimensional conceptualization of domestic violence (i.e., psychological aggression, physical assault, sexual coercion and injury), that interpersonal dependency is an important variable in predicting treatment completion and that the BIP significantly elevated the level of interpersonal dependency among treatment completers. Taken as a whole, the findings from this study provide initial empirical evidence for targeting dependency and attachment issues in BIPs treating women offenders. Importantly, in terms of placing dependency and attachment issues in the context of other explanatory theories, this discussion is not meant to imply that either dependency or attachment replace any of the existing theories regarding the development of abusive behaviors among women offenders. Rather, interpersonal dependency should be viewed as a complementary theory that adds a unique perspective to explaining the development of abusive behaviors among women in treatment for intimate partner violence.

LIMITATIONS

There are two drawbacks to this study that limit the conclusions that can be drawn from it and it is important to keep these limitations in mind when evaluating the findings. First, this study employed a sample of female batterers drawn from a predominately rural, southern state. It is clear that these batterers are not representative of female batterers in general and the results of this study may not be applicable to female batterers in different geographic regions and clinical settings. Second, as discussed previously, the predictive model is only useful for the women attending this particular treatment program. Other treatment programs around the country will have to develop their own models based on the characteristics of the women attending their treatment programs.

REFERENCES

Ainsworth, M. (1969). Object relations, dependency and attachment: A theoretical review of the infant-mother relationship. *Child Development, 40,* 969-1025.

Archer, J. (2000). Sex differences in aggression between heterosexual partners: A meta-analytic review. *Psychological Bulletin, 126,* 651-680.

Babcock, J., Miller, S., & Siard, C. (2003). Toward a typology of abusive women: Differences between partner-only and generally violent women in the use of violence. *Psychology of Women Quarterly, 27,* 153-161.

Bornstein, R. (1994). Construct validity of the Interpersonal Dependency Inventory: 1977-1992. *Journal of Personality Disorders, 8,* 64-76.

Bowlby, J. (1980). *Attachment and loss: Vol. 3 Loss, sadness and depression.* New York: Basic Books.

Busch, A., & Rosenberg, M. (2004). Comparing women and men arrested for domestic violence: A preliminary report. *Journal of Family Violence, 19,* 49-58.

Buttell, F., & Carney, M. (2002). Predictors of attrition among batterers court-ordered into treatment. *Social Work Research, 26,* 31-41.

Buttell, F., & Jones, C. (2001). Interpersonal dependency among court-ordered domestic violence offenders: A descriptive analysis. *Journal of Family Violence, 16,* 375-384.

Cadsky, O., Hanson, K., Crawford, M., & Lalonde, C. (1996). Attrition from a male batterer treatment program: Client-treatment congruence and lifestyle instability. *Violence and Victims, 11,* 51-64.

Carlsten, C. (2002). Literature is biased as studies rarely look at female to male violence. *British Medical Journal, 325,* 44.

Cazenave, N. A., & Straus, M. (1979). Race, class, network embeddedness and family violence: A search for potent support systems. *Journal of Comparative Family Studies, 10,* 281-299.

Daly, J., Power, T., & Gondolf, E. (2001). Predictors of batterer program attendance. *Journal of Interpersonal Violence, 16,* 971-991.

Davis, R., & Taylor, B. (1999). Does batterer treatment reduce violence? A synthesis of the literature. *Women and Criminal Justice, 10,* 69-93.

Davis, R., Taylor, B., & Maxwell, C. (1998). Does batterer treatment reduce violence? A randomized experiment in Brooklyn. *National Institute of Justice Final Report.* Washington, DC.

Dowd, L. (2001). Female perpetrators of partner aggression: Relevant issues and treatment. *Journal of Aggression, Maltreatment, & Trauma, 5,* 73-104.

Dunford, F. (2000). The San Diego Navy Experiment: An assessment of interventions for men who assault their wives. *Journal of Consulting and Clinical Psychology, 68,* 468-476.

DuRant, R., Cadenhead, C., Pendergrast, R., Slavens, G., & Linder, C. (1994). Factors associated with the use of violence among urban Black adolescents. *American Journal of Public Health, 84,* 612-617.

Dutton, D. (1995). *The batterer: A psychological profile.* New York: Basic Books.

Dutton, D. (2000). Witnessing parental violence as a traumatic experience shaping the abusive personality. *Journal of Aggression, Maltreatment & Trauma, 3,* 59-67.

Dwyer, D. (1999). Measuring domestic violence: An assessment of frequently used tools. *Journal of Offender Rehabilitation, 29,* 23-33.

Feder, L., & Forde, D. (2000). A test of the efficacy of court-mandated counseling for domestic violence offenders: The Broward experiment. *National Institute of Justice Final Report.* Washington, DC.

Fiebert, M., & Gonzalez, D. (1997). College women who initiate assaults on their male partners and the reasons offered for such behavior. *Psychological Reports, 80,* 583-590.

Gondolf, E. (1997). Batterer programs: What we know and need to know. *Journal of Interpersonal Violence, 12,* 83-98.

Hair, J. F., Jr., Anderson, R. E., Tatham, R. L., & Black, W. C. (1992). *Multivariate Data Analysis with Readings.* New York: Macmillan Publishing Company.

Hamberger, K. (1997). Female offenders in domestic violence: A look at actions in their context. *Journal of Aggression, Maltreatment & Trauma, 1,* 117-129.

Hamberger, K., & Hastings, J. (1988). Skills training for treatment of spouse abusers: An outcome study. *Journal of Family Violence, 3,* 121-130.

Hamberger, K., Lohr, J., & Bonge, D. (1994). Intended function of domestic violence is different for arrested male and female perpetrators. *Family Violence and Sexual Assault Bulletin, 10,* 40-44.

Hamberger, K., Lohr, J., & Gottlieb, M. (2000). Predictors of treatment dropout from a spouse abuse abatement program. *Behavior Modification, 24,* 528-552.

Hamberger, K., & Potente, T. (1994). Counseling heterosexual women arrested for domestic violence: Implications for theory and practice. *Violence and Victims, 9,* 125-137.

Hampton, R., Gelles, R., & Harrop, J. (1989). Is violence in Black families increasing? A comparison of 1975 and 1985 national survey rates. *Journal of Marriage and the Family, 51,* 969-980.

Henning, K., Jones, A., & Holdford, R. (2003). Treatment needs of women arrested for domestic violence: A comparison with male offenders. *Journal of Interpersonal Violence, 18,* 839-856.

Hirschfield, R., Klerman, G., Gough, H., Barrett, J., Korchin, S., & Chodoff, P. (1977). A measure of interpersonal dependency. *Journal of Personality Assessment, 41,* 610-618.

Holtzworth-Munroe, A., Bates, L., Smultzer, N., & Sandin, E. (1997). A brief review of the research on husband violence. *Aggression and Violent Behavior, 2,* 65-99.

Holtzworth-Munroe, A., Meehan, J., Herron, K., Rehman, U., & Stuart, G. (2000). Testing the Holtzworth-Munroe & Stuart (1994) batterer typology. *Journal of Consulting and Clinical Psychology, 68,* 1000-1019.

Kimmel, M. (2002). "Gender Symmetry" in domestic violence. *Violence Against Women, 8,* 1332-1363.

Lawson, D. (2003). Incidence, explanations, and treatment of partner violence. *Journal of Counseling and Development, 81,* 19-32.

Loeber, R., & Dishion, T. J. (1983). Early predictors of delinquency: A review. *Psychological Bulletin, 94,* 68-99.

Maiuro, R., Hagar, T., Lin, H., & Olson, N. (2001). Are current state standards for domestic violence perpetrator treatment adequately informed by research? A question of questions. *Journal of Aggression, Maltreatment & Trauma*, *5*, 21-44.

Martin, M. (1997). Double your trouble: Dual arrest in family violence. *Journal of Family Violence*, *12*, 139-157.

McNeely, R., Cook, P., & Torres, J. (2001). Is domestic violence a gender issue, or a human issue? *Journal of Human Behavior in the Social Environment*, *4*, 227-251.

Miller, S. (2001). The paradox of women arrested for domestic violence: Criminal justice professionals and service providers respond. *Violence Against Women*, *7*, 1339-1376.

Morse, B. (1995). Beyond the Conflict Tactics Scale: Assessing gender differences in partner violence. *Violence and Victims*, *10*, 251-272.

Murphy, C., Meyer, S., & O'Leary, D. (1994). Dependency characteristics of partner assaultive men. *Journal of Abnormal Psychology*, *103*, 729-735.

Pagelow, M. (1992). Adult victims of domestic violence: Battered women. *Journal of Interpersonal Violence*, *7*, 87-120.

Pirog-Good, M., & Stets-Kealey, J. (1986). Programs for abusers: Who drops out and what can be done. *Response*, *9*, 17-19.

Rennison, C., & Welchans, S. (2000). Intimate partner violence. *Bureau of Justice Statistics Report* (NCJ 178247). Washington, DC: U.S. Department of Justice.

Rosenbaum, A., & Leisring, P. (2001). Group intervention programs for men who batter. *Journal of Aggression, Maltreatment & Trauma*, *5*, 57-72.

Rosenbaum, A., & Leisring, P. (2003). Beyond power and control: Towards an understanding of partner abusive men. *Journal of Comparative Family Studies*, *34*, 7-22.

Rosenfeld, B. (1992). Court-ordered treatment of spouse abuse. *Clinical Psychology Review*, *12*, 205-226.

Saunders, D. (1996). Feminist-cognitive-behavioral and process-psychodynamic treatments for men who batter: Interactions of abuser traits and treatment model. *Violence and Victims*, *4*, 393-414.

Sonkin, D., & Dutton, D. (2003). Treating assaultive men from an attachment perspective. *Journal of Aggression, Maltreatment & Trauma*, *7*, 105-133.

Straus, M. (1979). Measuring intrafamily conflict and violence: The conflict tactics scales. *Journal of Marriage and the Family*, *41*, 75-88.

Straus, M. (1997). *Manual for the Conflict Tactics Scale (CTS)*. Durham, NH: University of New Hampshire.

Straus, M. (1999). Controversy over domestic violence by women: A methodological, theoretical, and sociology of science analysis. *National Institute of Mental Health Report* (NCJ 186243). Washington, DC: U.S. Department of Health and Human Services.

Straus, M., & Gelles, R. (1990). How violent are American families? Estimates from the national family violence resurvey and other and other studies. In M.A. Straus & R. Gelles, *Physical Violence in American Families: Risk Factors and Adaptations to Violence in 8,145 Families* (95-112). New Brunswick, NJ: Transaction Publishing.

Straus, M., Hamby, S., Boney-McCoy, S., Sugarman, D. (1996). The revised conflict tactics scales (CTS2): Development and preliminary psychometric data. *Journal of Family Issues*, *17*, 283-316.

Swan, S., & Snow, D. (2002). A typology of women's use of violence in intimate relationships. *Violence Against Women, 8*, 286-319.

Visher, C. A., Lattimore, P. K., & Linster, R. L. (1991). Predicting the recidivism of serious youthful offenders using survival models. *Criminology, 29*, 329-362.

Williams, O. (1992). Ethnically sensitive practice to enhance treatment participation of African-American men who batter. *Families in Society: The Journal of Contemporary Human Services, 73*, 588-595.

AUTHORS' NOTES

Michelle Mohr Carney, PhD, is Associate Professor in the School of Social Work at the University of Georgia in Athens, Georgia. Her primary research interests and expertise are in the areas of delinquent youth and batterer interventions, and evaluation research. She has conducted several evaluation studies, including evaluations of service provision for male and female batterers. She teaches graduate courses in macro practice (especially foundation and advanced community practice, development and non-profit administration), evaluation research, and case-based integrative seminars.

Frederick P. Buttell, PhD, LCSW, is Associate Professor in the School of Social Work at Tulane University in New Orleans, Louisiana. His primary research interests and expertise are in the areas of batterer interventions, research methods, and quantitative data analysis. Dr. Buttell has extensive clinical experience in providing court-mandated treatment services to batterers and he has investigated numerous aspects of batterer intervention programs. He has served as a training consultant to the Alabama Coalition Against Domestic Violence and the Women's Center at the University of Alabama and has evaluated aspects of service provision for male and female batterers. He teaches courses on advanced clinical practice and family development.

Address correspondence to Michelle Mohr Carney, PhD, Associate Professor, University of Georgia School of Social Work, 426 Tucker Hall, Athens, GA 30602 (E-mail: mmcarney@uga.edu).

Women Who Perpetrate Relationship Violence: Moving Beyond Political Correctness. Pp. 63-81.

Available online at http://www.haworthpress.com/web/JOR

doi:10.1300/J076v41n04_03

Personality Profiles of Women and Men Arrested for Domestic Violence: An Analysis of Similarities and Differences

CATHERINE A. SIMMONS
PETER LEHMANN
NORMAN COBB
CAROL R. FOWLER

ABSTRACT Women arrested for intimate partner violence raise challenges for those working in domestic violence programs. Theoretically, there is no agreement about whether women are aggressive for the same reasons as men or merely victims fighting back in an abusive relationship. Practically, there is very little research to guide treatment of this population. In the current exploratory study, Millon Clinical Multiaxial Inventory-III (MCMI-III) personality profiles of 78 females referred by the courts to a domestic violence diversion program were compared to those of a matched sample of 78 males referred by the courts to the same program. Compared with male offenders, women were more likely to demonstrate elevated histrionic, narcissistic, and compulsive personality traits, and less likely to demonstrate dependant personality traits. Additionally, women in this study were more likely to display MCMI-III profiles indicating the presence of personality disorders. Implications of these findings for the treatment setting are discussed. *[Article copies available for a fee from The Haworth Document Delivery Service: 1-800-HAWORTH. E-mail address: <docdelivery@haworthpress.com> Website: <http://www.HaworthPress.com> © 2005 by The Haworth Press, Inc. All rights reserved.]*

KEYWORDS Female batterers, domestic violence, personality profiles

INTRODUCTION

Despite the fact that domestic violence has been recognized as an important social problem for decades, the issue of women arrested for domestic violence related charges is only beginning to receive attention in the literature. To date, the majority of the articles published on this population argue that most (if not all) of the women arrested for domestic violence are not the primary aggressor but, instead, are victims fighting back (e.g., Cascardi & Vivian, 1995; Dobash, Dobash, Wilson, & Daly, 1992; Hamberger & Potente, 1994). However, a growing body of literature points to a sub-category of women arrested for domestic violence that do not fit into the traditional victim/self defense typology (e.g., Babcock, Miller, & Sirad, 2003; Stuart, Moore, Ramsey, & Kahler, 2003; Strauss & Gelles, 1986). In fact, a number of recent writings indicate that sometimes in domestic violence situations women are the primary aggressors (e.g., Bush & Rosenberg, 2004; McNeely, Cook, & Torris, 2001; Swan & Snow, 2002).

The sub-population of women arrested for partner violence who are the primary aggressor is an important population to research as they often present an interesting paradox to domestic violence treatment programs. Questions exist regarding whether female offenders should be (a) approached in the same manner as male offenders because of their similarities or (b) treated differently because they have inherently different personality structures and causes for their violence. One important step to answering some of these questions lies in understanding the basic personality structure of women arrested for partner violence and how it may differ from that of men arrested for partner violence. Even though the use of personality characteristics is controversial in the domestic violence literature and should not be used as the sole assessment of abusiveness (please see Dutton, 2003; Gondolf, 1999, 2003), understanding basic personality structures can shed light on how to best approach treatment initiatives. For this reason, the current study seeks to describe female batterers' personality traits relative to male batterers using the Millon Clinical Multiaxial Inventory-III (MCMI-III). Through understanding the similarities and differences in the personality profiles of male and female batterers, practical applications in the treatment settings can be developed.

Debate About Women as Batterers

The idea that females can be the primary aggressor in domestic violence situations is quite controversial. Over 25 years ago, Strauss (1977-1978) first reported findings from the National Family Violence Survey that indicated women use violence as often as men in intimate relationships. At that time, his findings were rejected by some, replicated by others, and debated by many (Pearson, 1997). Given these mixed reviews, experts in the field of intimate partner violence have continued to disagree as to whether women's use of intimate violence is comparable to men's. Currently, two divergent views exist.

On one side of the debate are those who believe that male and female use of intimate violence differs both qualitatively and quantitatively (e.g., Dobash, Dobash, Wilson, & Daly, 1992; Hamberger & Potente, 1994; Schwartz & DeKeseredy, 1997). For those with this point of view, domestic violence is a result of the patriarchal difference in power between men and women. That is, men batter women because they are privileged physically, financially, and socially (Mills, 2003). It is argued that many if not most women arrested for intimate partner violence are victims of abuse themselves who may be acting in self-defense (e.g., Hamberger & Potente; Hamby & Sugarman, 1999; Miller, 2001). Theoretically, this is different from male offenders whose violence is more often related to power and control issues (Dobash & Dobash, 1979), pathological personalities (Craig, 2003), and/or concerns about abandonment (Dutton, 1999). Those who subscribe to this view believe women arrested for intimate violence are the victims and very rarely, if ever, the true offenders.

On the other side of the debate are those who contend that, in intimate partner situations, male and female use of violence is similar (e.g., Adams, 2000; McNeeley & Mann, 1990; McNeeley & Robinson-Simpson, 1987; Shupe, Stacy, & Hazelwood, 1987; Steinmetz, 1977-1978; Strauss, 1993; Strauss, Gelles, & Steinmetz, 1980). From this perspective, it is argued that women both (a) use violence in their relationships as frequently as men (e.g., Archer, 2000; Strauss, 1993; Strauss, Gelles, & Steinmetz, 1980) and (b) use violence for the same reasons as men (e.g., Bush & Rosenberg, 2004; McNeely et al., 2001; McNeeley & Mann, 1990; Shupe, Stacy, & Hazelwood, 1987; Steinmetz, 1977-1978). Theoretically, women are viewed as being both as capable and as likely as men of being the aggressor in domestic violence situations. Those who subscribe to this stance believe that, in domestic violence situations, women are sometimes the victims, sometimes the offenders, and sometimes both.

Prevalence of Female Arrests

Regardless of individual opinion, there is no doubt that violence by women does in fact occur. Female offenders account for 22% of all arrests in the United States, 15% of all domestic violence related arrests, and 4% of all male homicides (Rennison, 2003). Although some argue that female domestic violence arrests are the result of mandatory pro-arrest laws designed to protect women (e.g., Mignon & Holmes, 1995; Victim Services Agency, 1989), the fact remains that women continue to be arrested on charges related to partner violence. Once involved in the criminal justice system, these women are often referred to domestic violence treatment programs where gender specific therapeutic options are limited due to scant literature available on this population.

Personality Profiles Using the MCMI-III

Personality profiles, such as the MCMI-III, are useful tools in treating domestic violence offenders (Craig, 2003) even though no one "abuse profile" exists (Beasley & Stoltenberg, 1992). Currently, very little literature is published on the personality profiles of female batterers; however, a number of studies with male batterers have used MCMI profiles (e.g., Craig, 2003; Gondolf, 1999; Retzlaff, Stoner, & Kleinsasser, 2002). From these studies, an understanding of the differing batterers' personalities has begun to be understood.

Although it has been suggested that as much as 80% of men who batter demonstrate personality disorders, further research indicates this estimate is quite high (Gondolf, 1999). Based on these varying findings, recent publications recommend that mental health professionals working with domestic violence offenders look at personality styles instead of personality disorders to help define treatment options (Craig, 2003). "Personality styles reflect deeply etched and pervasive characteristics of functioning that perpetuate and aggravate everyday difficulties" (Millon, 1997, p. 15). They are so embedded and automatic that the individual is often unaware of self-destructive consequences (Millon, 1997). By understanding the personality styles most prevalent in batterers, treatment programs can more effectively define treatment options that will be successful (Craig, 2003).

A number of studies have used personality tests to assess the personality structure of men arrested for intimate partner violence (e.g., Craig, 2003; Gondolf, 1999; Retzlaff, Stoner, & Kleinsasser, 2002). From these the personality traits antisocial, aggressive-sadistic, passive-aggressive (negativistic), and narcissistic appear most frequently on the MCMI profiles of men (Craig, 2003). In spite of the number of studies assessing the personality styles of male batterers, only one published article (Henning, Jones, & Holdford, 2003) and one published dissertation (Fowler, 2002) have used personality testing to assess the personality structures of female batterers. Different from the characteristics found in males arrested for partner violence, females arrested for partner violence were found to demonstrate compulsive, histrionic, and narcissistic personality traits (Fowler, 2002; Henning et al., 2003).

Purpose of the Current Study

The purpose of the current exploratory study is to gain a greater understanding of women arrested for partner violence through examining their personality styles and comparing them to the personality styles of males arrested for partner violence. Findings from four previous studies indicate that women use violence for different reasons than men (Abel, 2001; Hamberger & Potente, 1994; Henning & Feder, 2004; Henning et al., 2003). From these studies' findings that women arrested for intimate partner violence are not similar to men arrested for intimate partner violence, the following two hypotheses were tested: (1) Women who are in treatment for intimate partner violence will have different personality styles than men who are in treatment for intimate partner violence as defined by MCMI-III subscales $\geq$ Base Rate (BR) 60. (2) Women who are in treatment for intimate partner violence will have higher levels of likely personality dysfunction than men who are in treatment for intimate partner violence as defined by MCMI-III subscales $\geq$ BR 85. Consistent with previous studies (Fowler, 2002; Henning et al., 2003), we expected women would demonstrate higher response elevations than men on the following MCMI-III subscales: Compulsive, Histrionic, and Narcissistic.

METHODOLOGY

Data Collection

Subjects for this study are 156 court-ordered participants seen between 1999 and 2004 in the Diversion Program located at the University of Texas at Arlington Community Service Clinic in Arlington, Texas. Consent to release information forms were signed by all of the participants prior to completion of their intake paperwork that included the MCMI-III. The female group consists of all 78 of the women enrolled in the program who signed consent to release information forms. The male group consists of 78 of the 567 males participating in the program matched to the female participants on ethnicity (50% Caucasian, 25% African American, 20% Hispanic, 2.5% Asian and 2.5% other), age (mean age = 30.44 yrs) and income (mean income between $20,000 and $29,999/yr).

Measurement Tool

MCMI-III: The MCMI-III (Millon, 1997), the second major revision of the MCMI, is a widely used, 175-item, true-false inventory with 5 sets of scales, including (a) 11 Personality Disorder Scales (Schizoid, Avoidant, Depressive, Dependant, Histrionic, Narcissistic, Antisocial, Aggressive, Compulsive, Negativistic, and Masochistic), (b) 3 Severe Personality Disorder Scales (Schizotypal, Borderline, and Paranoid), (c) 7 Clinical Syndrome Scales (Anxiety, Somatic, Manic, Dysthymic, Alcohol, Drug, and PTSD), (d) 3 Severe Syndrome Scales (Thought Disorder, Major Depression, and Delusional), and (e) 3 Validity Scales (Disclosure, Desirability, and Debasement). Subjects with MCMI-III Validity Scale Scores that suggested the response pattern for the remainder of the subscales was suspect and therefore invalid were not considered for this study (Millon).

Both individual items on the MCMI-III and the subscales they encompass reflect diagnostic criteria established by the DSM-IV (Millon, 1997). MCMI-III Clinical Syndrome Scales and Severe Syndrome Scales generally reflect DSM-IV Axis I criteria and MCMI-III Personality Disorder Scales and Severe Personality Disorder Scales generally reflect DSM-IV Axis II criteria. Cutoff scores on the MCMI-III were established through response pattern comparison of 998 males and females known to have the disorders included in each subscale and adjusted to accommodate gender differences in response style. When interpreting MCMI-III scores $\geq$ BR 60 indicates personality styles while scores $\geq$ BR 85 indicates clinical disorders (Millon).

Data Analysis

A two-step process was used to analyze the MCMI-III results of the current study. First, individual subscales meeting clinical significance for personality style ($\geq$ BR 60) and personality disorder ($\geq$ BR 85) were compared using frequencies and percentages. Next, the mean comparisons were tested using the individual sample two-way *t* test to determine differences in the overall profiles of 156 participants (78 female and 78 male) in the University of Texas at Arlington Community Service Clinic's Domestic Violence Diversion Program. Invalid profiles were discarded from the population prior to the subject matching process.

Table 1 summarizes the percentage of subjects who demonstrated cutoff scores $\geq$ BR 60 and $\geq$ BR 85 on each of the clinical subscales. These percentages indicate the proportion of the sample that showed elevated scores in each area. An extremely high proportion of female respondents indicate personality traits (scores $\geq$ BR 60) in three areas (a) compulsive (74.3%), (b) histrionic (74.3%), and (c) narcissistic (71.4%). Although a considerable proportion of males also indicated similar traits (compulsive 46.1%, histrionic 25.6%, and narcissistic 47.4%), the proportion of the female population who indicated these personality traits is considerably greater than the percent of male respondents indicating similar profiles. Graph 1 illustrates these differences in greater detail. Correspondingly, all of the subjects in this study demonstrated clinically significant levels on 2 or more of the 14 MCMI-III personality subscales, indicating a high presence of clinically significant personality traits ($\geq$ BR 60) in both the female and the male batterer populations.

Additionally, a number of the men and women comprising this sample show clinically significant personality traits, with 25.6% (20) of the males and 70.5% (55) of the females scoring high ($\geq$ BR 85) in at least one subscale, therefore indicating an elevated likelihood of personality disorders. In the female sample, personality disorders (individuals with MCMI-III scores $\geq$ BR 85 on at least one personality subscale) are almost three times as likely as in the male sample. The subscales avoidant (8.9%), narcissistic (6.4%), dependant (5.1%), and negativistic (5.1%) were the most frequently occurring personality disorders (score $\geq$ BR 85) for the males while the subscales histrionic (24.3%), compulsive (21.7%), and dependant (10.2%) were the most frequently occurring personality disorders (score $\geq$ BR 85) for the females.

Results of the two-way independent sample *t* tests found in Table 2 indicate that there is no significant difference between the males and females on 23 of the 27 MCMI-III subscales (see Table 2). However, the Compulsive subscale ($t = -4.252$, $df = 154$, $p = .000$), the Histrionic subscale ($t = -5.400$, $df = 154$, $p = .000$), and the Narcissistic subscale ($t = -1.978$, $df = 154$, $p = .050$) meet significance at the .05 level indicating

☐ **Table 1: Frequencies of MCMI-III scores that meet clinical significance.**

	% males > 60	% females > 60	% males > 84	% females > 84
Schizoid	32.0%	29.4%	0.0%	1.2%
Avoidant	41.0%	26.9%	8.9%	5.1%
Depressive	29.4%	25.6%	1.2%	1.2%
Dependant	44.8%	24.3%	5.1%	10.2%
Histrionic	25.6%	74.3%	1.2%	24.3%
Narcissistic	47.4%	71.4%	6.4%	7.6%
Antisocial	29.4%	33.3%	2.5%	2.5%
Sadistic	33.3%	33.3%	0.0%	2.5%
Compulsive	46.1%	74.3%	0.0%	21.7%
Negativistic	35.8%	26.9%	5.1%	2.5%
Masochistic	29.4%	25.6%	1.2%	7.6%
Schizotypal	34.6%	23.0%	1.2%	0.0%
Borderline	32.0%	24.3%	1.2%	1.2%
Paranoid	44.8%	39.7%	2.5%	2.5%
Anxiety	43.5%	39.7%	5.1%	1.2%
Somatoform	30.7%	25.6%	0.0%	0.0%
Bipolar	52.5%	52.5%	1.2%	0.0%
Dysthymia	41.0%	19.2%	1.2%	1.2%
Alcohol Dependence	42.3%	65.3%	5.1%	1.2%
Drug Dependence	16.6%	35.8%	0.0%	2.5%
PTSD	23.0%	29.4%	0.0%	0.0%
Thought Disorder	24.3%	16.6%	1.2%	0.0%
Major Depression	20.5%	20.5%	1.2%	3.8%
Delusional Disorder	48.7%	35.8%	0.0%	0.0%

that the females experience these personality traits more frequently than the males. Additionally, the Dependant subscale ($t = 2.055$, $df = 154$ $p = .042$) meets significance at the .05 level, indicating that the males experience this personality trait more frequently than the females.

Even though both the males and the females demonstrate high desirability scores on the MCMI-III (M males = 75.38, M females = 70.77), all of the profiles used were considered valid by MCMI standards. Graph 2 outlines the mean female MCMI-III profile for the sample. The

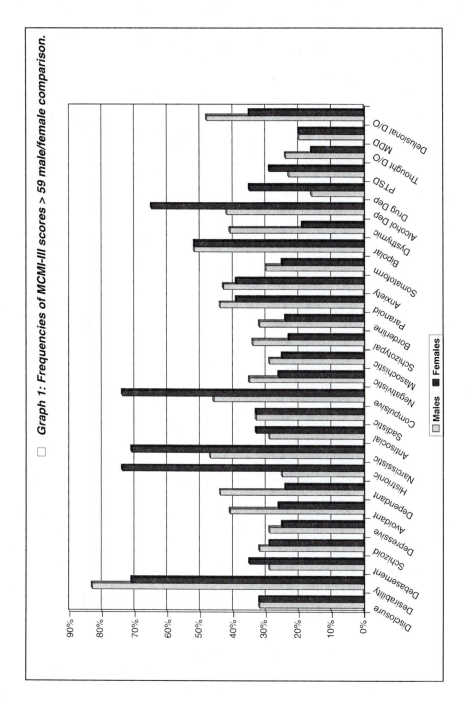

Graph 1: Frequencies of MCMI-III scores > 59 male/female comparison.

71

☐ **Table 2: Gender comparisons of means, percentage of clinically significant clients, t test and ANOVA results.**

	mean male	mean female	2-way t test	P
Schizoid	38.04	35.74	0.540	.590
Avoidant	39.33	33.78	1.262	.209
Depressive	41.90	32.14	1.892	.060
Dependant	50.45	41.78	2.055	.042*
Histrionic	53.18	69.03	−5.400	.000*
Narcissistic	60.26	65.36	−1.978	.050*
Antisocial	42.22	39.62	0.668	.505
Sadistic	36.68	34.14	0.625	.533
Compulsive	58.35	69.87	−4.252	.000*
Negativistic	38.78	32.23	1.393	.166
Masochistic	31.35	33.60	−0.461	.646
Schizotypal	33.59	27.78	1.306	.193
Borderline	35.36	30.64	0.818	.318
Paranoid	40.54	36.55	0.780	.381
Anxiety	39.97	38.95	0.184	.854
Somatoform	26.64	27.24	−0.133	.894
Bipolar	47.27	48.22	−0.257	.797
Dysthymia	33.23	26.41	1.433	.154
Alcohol Dep.	44.82	47.35	−0.607	.545
Drug Dep.	37.31	34.88	0.618	.538
PTSD	28.04	30.15	−0.481	.631
Thought	33.06	25.10	1.898	.060
Maj. Dep.	28.28	27.05	0.269	.789
Delusional	37.92	29.45	1.862	.065

* $p < .05$

mean score profile of the female sample indicates high scores in the Narcissistic ($M = 65.36$), Histrionic ($M = 69.03$), and Compulsive ($M = 68.87$) personality style categories. These elevated rates are consistent with the percentage of individuals demonstrating clinically significant personality traits, Compulsive (74.3%), Histrionic (74.3%), and Narcissistic (71.7%). Additionally, the entire population scored relatively low

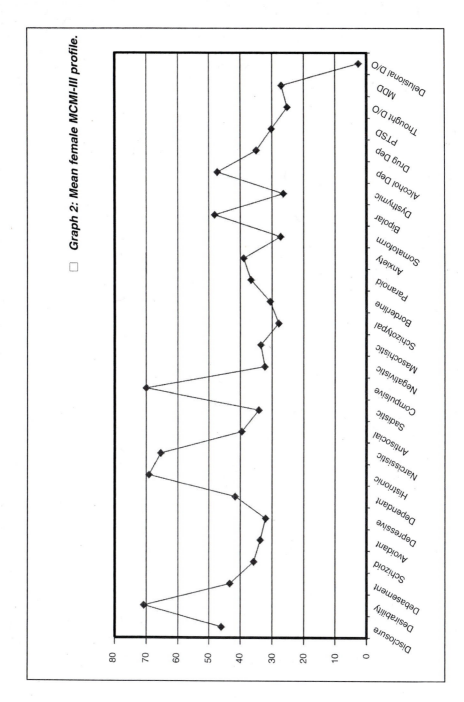

□ *Graph 2: Mean female MCMI-III profile.*

on the subscales more frequently found in males: (a) Antisocial (males mean = 42.22, females mean = 39.62), (b) Aggressive-Sadistic (males mean = 36.68, females mean = 34.14), and (c) Passive-Aggressive/Negativistic (males mean = 38.78, females mean = 32.23).

DISCUSSION

Two main implications for working with women arrested for domestic violence arise from the current exploratory study. The first is that personality profiles of males arrested for partner violence and females arrested for partner violence appear to be different. The second is that women court ordered to the domestic violence diversion program are likely to demonstrate high compulsive, histrionic, and narcissistic personality traits. By understanding differences in the personality profiles of females who use interpersonal violence, treatment options for women seen in domestic violence treatment programs can be improved.

Gender Differences

The personality profile most frequently indicated by women in this exploratory study is different from both (a) the personality profiles demonstrated by men in the current study and (b) male batterer personality traits noted in the literature. Women demonstrated elevated histrionic, narcissistic, and compulsive personality traits when compared to the matched sample of men while the men demonstrated higher dependant personality traits than the women in the study. These differences are significant in so far as the t-test findings and in the extremely high percentage of women who demonstrated scores ≥ BR 60 in these three areas (compulsive 74.3%, histrionic 74.3%, and narcissistic 71.4%). Likewise, findings from the current female sample are also different from the antisocial, aggressive-sadistic, passive-aggressive (negativistic), and narcissistic traits that appear most frequently on the MCMI profiles of men (Craig, 2003). These noted differences seem to suggest the personality profiles of women in domestic violence treatment differ greatly from those of men in domestic violence treatment.

In addition to differences in personality profiles, the females sampled demonstrated a higher percentage of likely personality disorders than the males in the sample (70.5% vs. 25.6%). Although it is important to note that personality disorders are not generally diagnosed using the MCMI-III alone, individuals with a score ≥ BR 85 are more likely to be diagnosed with an Axis II disorder (Millon, 1997). For this reason, MCMI-III scores are commonly used to measure personality disorders in the domestic violence literature (Gondolf, 1999) and are used in this context to indicate a likelihood of pathological personality.

Differences noted in the current study are congruent with those in the literature regarding the presence of personality disorders among domestically violent men and women. Finding a relatively high percentage of the female sample with likely personality disorders (70.5%) is similar to the work of Henning et al. (2003) who identified personality disorder profiles in 95% of their domestically violent female subjects. The lower overall percentage of females having potential personality disorders when compared with Henning et al.'s work (70.5% vs. 95%) is most likely the result of using different cutoff scores. The current study uses the ≥ BR 85 to indicate a personality disorder profile whereas Henning and colleagues used the ≥ BR 75 cutoff criterion. Likewise, finding a low percentage of men with likely personality disorders is congruent with the work of Gondolf (1999), who discovered a lower-than-expected percentage of male personality disorders among the male batterers comprising his sample.

Personality Profiles

Finding that high levels of histrionic, narcissistic, and compulsive personality traits are present in the female sample is consistent with two previous studies of females arrested for partner violence that utilize the MCMI-III (Fowler, 2002; Henning et al., 2003). As illustrated in Table 1, more than 70% of the women demonstrate BR scores ≥ 60 for these three subscales, indicating a high presence of histrionic, narcissistic, and compulsive personality traits in the female sample. These findings are similar to those of Henning et al., who found the percentage of women with BR scores ≥ 75 to be 50% for compulsive, 36.6% for histrionic, and 33% for narcissistic. Similarities between the findings of the current study and past work serve to validate the presence of these personality styles in the population of women in treatment for partner violence and therefore should be examined within the context of using violence in interpersonal relationships.

Initially, the three personality styles histrionic, narcissistic, and compulsive may appear contradictory. One may question how these individuals can constantly and voraciously seek attention from others (histrionic) while over-valuing themselves and requiring little social approval (narcissistic), even as they conform to the demands of others, experiencing underlying hostility at having to do so (compulsive). The fact that these women are all court ordered to attend a domestic violence diversion program may explain these apparent contradictions, particularly regarding the compulsive personality element. Women mandated to batterer intervention programs may utilize coping mechanisms that are congruent with compulsive personality traits, including denying their problems, not assuming responsibility for their own actions, blaming others, minimizing their own roles in the situations they find themselves in, and justifying and rationalizing their violent actions (Anderson, 1995; Wexler, 2000).

Regarding the histrionic and narcissistic personality elements of the findings, what these two personality styles share in common is a distinct disregard for other's thoughts and/or emotions, with a tendency to see others as being there for their own needs and uses. When the needs of both the histrionic and narcissistic individual are not met, they may act out their feelings of anger and rage in the form of physical violence (Millon, 1997). Therefore, it could be posited that this study's group of women with histrionic and/or narcissistic tendencies may find themselves using physical violence when they perceive that others (e.g., intimate partners) are not meeting their emotional needs. Physical violence may be utilized as a method to regain control (i.e., having their needs/expectations met) when other methods are unsuccessful (e.g., coercion, and/or manipulation).

Implications

When discussing the implications of findings from the current study it is important to remember that individuals arrested for domestic violence are not a homogeneous group. Males and females in domestic violence treatment have different personality traits and different treatment needs. Therefore, the current one-size-fits-all approach that many treatment programs use is not recommended for all women presenting to these programs (Holtzworth-Munroe & Stuart, 1994). This may be particularly important as the increase in female arrests leads to subsequent referrals to domestic violence treatment (Clifford, 1999).

Implications from the findings of (a) elevated histrionic, narcissistic, and compulsive personality styles and (b) higher-than-expected personality disorder profiles among the women in this sample suggest that women arrested for intimate partner violence and court ordered to treatment are likely to have long-standing personality and/or interpersonal issues that may complicate all aspects of their lives. Addressing this in the treatment setting through helping domestically violent females improve both (a) their interpersonal coping skills and (b) their ability to regulate emotions may serve to improve treatment of the female batterer population.

Limitations

A major limitation of this study is the mandated nature of the subjects. There is the possibility that the women included in this study represent the end of a continuum of women who are brought to the legal system's awareness through domestic violence arrest and prosecution. Consequently these women may be interpreted as the most serious or worst cases (i.e., the women who are found to be the "obvious" or apparently sole perpetrators by responding police officers to domestic violence calls and the referring court personnel). Given society's and the criminal justice system's continuing maintenance of stereotypes that women are almost always victims of domestic violence, it is likely that without obvious and incontrovertible evidence that a woman was a primary perpetrator, the male partner is more likely to be arrested for a domestic violence incident that may have been mutually violent (Pearson, 1997).

An additional limitation of the current research is related to the potential males in domestic violence treatment programs have for minimizing their behaviors in the treatment setting. Mainstream feminists hold that men who batter have a chronic pattern of minimizing symptoms of their abusive behavior (Mills, 2003). These beliefs are supported by research that indicates men report that they inflict fewer injuries on their female partners and participate in lower levels of violence than women report (e.g., Browning, & Dutton, 1986). Despite the potential for male subjects to minimize their use of violence, there was no significant difference between the two groups on the MCMI-III Desirability Scale. From the lack of difference on this scale it must be assumed that the two groups reported similar levels of truthfulness on their tests and the findings are valid.

Additional Research

Given the limitations of this study, the importance of additional research in the area of serving women arrested for domestic violence is highlighted. Of greatest interest are (a) follow-ups with treatment pro-

viders who see women, particularly to address whether re-arrest has occurred and to what extent (if any) violence still exists, (b) rigorous
evaluation research with women in various stages of the identification
and treatment process, and (c) development of theory driven models to
test the treatment efficacy for this unique female population. Attention
to these issues is important because inclusion of females arrested for intimate partner violence with high levels of histrionic, narcissistic, and
compulsive personality traits and/or the presence of personality disorders in trauma recovery programs and victims services may encourage
rationalization, therefore increasing recidivism. Likewise, inclusion of
females who do not display these personality traits and are instead "victims fighting back" in the traditional male treatment groups may cause
re-victimization when more appropriate treatment might be trauma services, assertiveness training, and/or developing a net of safety for self
and family. Because either mistake is harmful to both the client and to
her intimate partner, the importance of careful treatment planning with
this population is further emphasized. Using personality profiles in domestic violence treatment programs can help to distinguish between
those women who are truly victims fighting back (e.g., Hamberger &
Potente, 1994) and those who are the true aggressors in their
relationships (e.g., Strauss, 1993), thereby improving treatment for
these women.

REFERENCES

Abel, E. (2001). Comparing the social service utilization, exposure to violence , and
    trauma symptomology of domestic violence female "victims" and female
    "batterers." *Journal of Family Violence*, 16(4), 401-420.
Adams, S.R. (2000). Understanding women who are violent in intimate relationships:
    Implications for Army Family Advocacy. *Military Medicine*, 165(3), 214-218.
Archer, J. (2000). Sex differences in aggression between heterosexual partners: A
    meta-analytic review. *Psychology Bulletin*, 126(5), 651-680.
Anderson, G. (1995). *A ray of hope: A guide to interpersonal relationships*. Los An-
    geles, CA: Anderson & Anderson, APC.
Babcock, J.C., Miller, S.A., & Sirad, C. (2003). Toward a typology of abusive women:
    Differences between partner only and generally violent women in the use of vio-
    lence. *Psychology of Women Quarterly*, 27(2), 153-161.
Beasley, R., & Stolenberg, C.D. (1992). Personality characteristics of male spouse
    abusers. *Professional Psychology: Research and Practice*, 23(4), 310-317.
Browning, J., & Dutton, D.G. (1986). Assessment of wife assault with the Conflicts
    Tactic Scale: Using couples data to quantify the differential reporting effect. *Jour-
    nal of Marriage and Family*, 48, 375-379.

Busch, A.L., & Rosenberg, M.S. (2004). Comparing women and men arrested for Domestic Violence: A preliminary report. *Journal of Family Violence*, 19(1), 49-57.

Cascardi, M., & Vivian, D. (1995). Context for specific episodes of marital violence: Gender and severity of violence differences. *Journal of Family Violence*, 10(3), 265-293.

Clifford, J.O. (1999, November 26). Arrests of women increase under Calif. domestic violence law. *The Washington Post*, p. A11.

Craig, R.J. (2003). Use of Millon Clinical Multiaxial Inventory in the psychological assessment of domestic violence: A review. *Aggression and Violent Behavior*, 8(3), 235-243.

Dobash R., & Dobash, R.E. (1979). *Violence against wives: A case against patriarchy.* New York: Free Press.

Dobash, R., Dobash, R.E., Wilson, M., & Daly, M. (1992). The myth of sexual symmetry in marital violence. *Social Problems*, 39, 71-91.

Dutton, D. (1999). The traumatic origins of intimate rage. *Aggression and Violent Behavior*, 4(4), 431-448.

Dutton, D. (2003). MCMI results for batterers: A response to Gondolf. *Journal of Family Violence*, 18(4), 253-255.

Fowler, C.R. (2002). *Intimate violence: A comparison of female and male court-mandated batters*, Unpublished doctoral dissertation. California School of Professional Psychology, Fresno.

Gondolf, E.W. (1999). MCMI-III results for batterers program participants in four cities: Less "pathological" than expected. *Journal of Family Violence*, 14(1), 1-17.

Gondolf, E.W. (2003). MCMI results for batterers: Gondolf replies to Dutton's response. *Journal of Family Violence*, 18(6), 387-389.

Hamberger, K., & Potente, T. (1994). Counseling heterosexual women arrested for domestic violence: Implications for theory and practice. *Violence and Victims*, 9(2), 125-137.

Hamby, S.L., & Sugarman, D.B. (1999). Acts of psychological aggression against partner and their relation to physical assault and gender. *Journal of Marriage and the Family*, 61, 959-970.

Henning, K., Jones, A., & Holdford, R. (2003). Treatment needs of women arrested for domestic violence: A comparison with male offenders. *Journal of Interpersonal Violence*, 18(8), 839-856.

Henning, K., & Feder, L. (2004). A comparison between men and women arrested for domestic violence: Who presents the greater threat? *Journal of Family Violence*.

Holtzworth-Munroe, A., & Stuart, G.L. (1994). Typologies of male batterers: Three subtypes and the differences among them. *Psychological Bulletin*, 116(3), 476-497.

McNeely, R.L., Cook, P.W., & Torres, J.B. (2001). Is domestic violence a gender issue, or a human issue? *Journal of Human Behavior in the Social Environment*, 4(4), 227-251.

McNeely, R.L., & Mann, C.R., (1990). Domestic violence is a human issue. *Journal of International Violence*, 5(1), 129-132.

McNeely, R.L., & Robinson-Simpson, G. (1987). The truth about domestic violence: A falsely framed issue. *Social Work*, 32(2), 485-490.

Mignon, S., & Holmes, W. (1995). Police response to mandatory arrest laws. *Crime & Delinquency*, 41(4), 430-443.

Miller, S.L. (2001). The paradox of women arrested for domestic violence. *Violence Against Women*, 7(12), 1339-1376.

Millon, T. (1997). *Millon Clinical Multiaxial Inventory-III: manual* (2nd ed.). Minneapolis, MN: National Computer Systems.

Mills, L.G. (2003). *Insult to injury; Rethinking our responses to intimate abuse.* Princeton: Princeton University Press.

Pearson, P. (1997). *When she was bad; Violent women and the myth of innocence.* New York: Viking Penguin.

Rennison, C.M. (2002). Intimate partner violence, 1993-2001, *Bureau of Justice Statistics Crime Data Brief.* Washington, DC: U.S. Department of Justice.

Retzlaff, P., Stoner, J., & Kleinsasser, D. (2002). The use of the MCMI-III in the screening and triage of offenders. *International Journal of Offender Therapy and Comparative Criminology*, 46(3), 319-322.

Schwartz, W.S., & DeKeseredy, W.S. (1997). *Sexual assault on the college campus: The role of male peer support.* Thousand Oaks, CA: Sage.

Shupe, A., Stacy, W.A., & Hazelwood, L.R. (1987). *Violent men, violent couples: The dynamics of domestic violence.* Lexington, MA: Lexington Books.

Steinmetz, S.K. (1977-1978). The battered husband syndrome. *Victimology*, 2(3-sup-4), 499-493.

Strauss, M. (1977-1978). Wife beating: How common and why? *Victimology: An International Journal*, 2(3-sup-4), 443-458.

Strauss, M.A. (1993). Physical assaults by wives: A major social problem. In R.J. Gelles & D.R. Losske (Eds.), *Current controversies on family violence* (pp. 67-87). Newbury Park, CA: Sage.

Strauss, M.A., Gelles, R.J., & Steinmetz, S.K. (1980). *Behind closed doors: Violence in the American family.* Garden City, NY: Doubleday.

Stuart, G.L., Moore, T.M., Ramsey, S.E., & Kahler, C.W. (2003). Relationship aggression and substance use among women court-referred to domestic violence intervention programs. *Addictive Behaviors*, 28, *Special Issue: Interpersonal Violence and Substance Use*, 1603-1610.

Swan & Snow (2002). A typology of women's use of violence in intimate relationships. *Violence Against Women*, 8(3), 75-109.

Wexler, D. B. (2000). *Domestic violence 2000: An integrated skills program for men. Group leader's manual.* New York, NY: W. W. Norton & Company.

Victim Services Agency (1989). State legislation providing for law enforcement response to family violence. *Response*, 12(3), 6-9.

AUTHORS' NOTES

Catherine A. Simmons, LCSW, BCD, is a PhD candidate at the University of Texas at Arlington School of Social Work. Her research interests include women's experiences with traumatic events, PTSD, and women's use of violence.

Peter Lehmann, PhD, LCSW, is Associate Professor at the University of Texas at Arlington School of Social Work and the director of the Community Service Clinic. His research interests include PTSD research with women and children, women's issues, and clinical practice.

Norman Cobb, PhD, LCSW, is Associate Professor at the University of Texas at Arlington School of Social Work and formerly the director of the Community Service Clinic. His research interests include social work ethics, professional behavior, and domestic violence.

Carol R. Fowler, PhD, is a practicing psychologist currently serving in the United States Air Force. Her research interests focus on female use of violence and forensics.

Address correspondence to Catherine A. Simmons, LCSW, BCD, 706 Walnut Valley Lane, Cordova, TN 38018 (E-mail: cas0558@exchange.uta.edu).

Women Who Perpetrate Relationship Violence: Moving Beyond Political Correctness. Pp. 83-98.

Available online at http://www.haworthpress.com/web/JOR

doi:10.1300/J076v41n04_04

Women as the Aggressors in Intimate Partner Homicide in Houston, 1980s to 1990s

VICTORIA B. TITTERINGTON
LAURA HARPER

ABSTRACT *Objective:* The purpose of this study was to inform the ongoing quest for efficacious treatment of domestically violent women by (a) describing their representation in cases of intimate partner homicide over the period of 1985-1999 in Houston, Texas, and (b) by utilizing a measure known as the spousal sex ratio of killing (SROK), determining variation in this female offending by race/ethnicity and whether the relationship was registered or *defacto*.

Method: Secondary data from the Houston police department homicide division murder logs and the U.S. Bureau of the Census were analyzed to determine the incidence and proportion of women's perpetration of intimate partner homicide.

Results: Throughout the fifteen-year period of this study, women were over 40 percent of the offenders in lethal domestic assaults. Both victims and offenders in these intimate partner incidents were disproportionately Black. When comparing the sex ratios of killing by racial/ethnic subgroups, Black women were equally (or more) likely than Black men to be the perpetrators of intimate domestic homicide. Among non-Hispanic Whites (including Asians, others), there were 63 female intimate partner homicide offenders for every 100 male offenders. Within the small number of cases involving Hispanic couples, women were much more likely to be the aggressors in intimate partner homicide in the latter time period of this investigation. For both Blacks and Whites women were more likely to be the perpetrators in non-marital dyads.

Conclusion: Implications of these findings for criminal justice and social service practitioners are discussed. *[Article copies available for a fee from The Haworth Document Delivery Service: 1-800-HAWORTH. E-mail address: <docdelivery@haworthpress.com> Website: <http://www.HaworthPress.com> © 2005 by The Haworth Press, Inc. All rights reserved.]*

KEYWORDS Intimate partner homicide, domestic violence

INTRODUCTION

Intimacy is perhaps the most important feature of human interaction, but it can also be the most volatile. In recent years, much research has focused on the problem of intimate partner violence, especially when that violence culminates in the death of one or both of the partners, yet intimate homicide is not a recent phenomenon. The sociologist Emile Durkheim once wrote that, "While family life has a moderating effect upon suicide, it rather stimulates murder" (1897:354). Although it may not be the case that married life *induces* homicidal violence, it is obvious that such occurrences are a challenge for the criminal justice system, as well as for social services and domestic violence agencies. For the period of the present study (1985-1999), there were, on average, 2,155 intimate partner homicide victims annually in the U.S. (Federal Bureau of Investigation Multiple years). According to a U.S. Department of Justice study, in the twenty-year period between 1976 and 1996, six out of every 100 male homicide victims and thirty of every 100 female victims were killed at the hands of their intimate partners (Greenfeld et al., 1998).

Since the passage of the federal Violence against Women Act of 1994, an abundance of research literature has emerged regarding women's representation as victims of both non-lethal and lethal domestic violence. But we also know that, for the period of the present investigation (1985-1999), females nationally were offenders rather than victims in an average of 33 percent of cases each year (FBI Multiple years). In other words, when a woman does kill someone, it often takes place in the home, against an intimate (Browne & Williams, 1993). The prevalence of such violence makes it important that we gain a more detailed understanding of female, as well as male, domestic homicide perpetrators.

Research conducted using the FBI's Supplemental Homicide Reports has shown a number of generalized national trends concerning intimate partner homicide. While numerically the majority of these victims are White or Hispanic, the homicide rate is considerably higher for Blacks (Riedel & Best, 1998), who are found to be at a much higher risk than other groups to be killed by their partners (Mercy & Saltzman, 1989). For example, in 1995 in Los Angeles, California, Riedel and Lewitt (1998) found that the intimate partner homicide rate for Blacks was 51.4 per 100,000, whereas Whites had a rate of only 5.4.

The present paper offers a more precise description of the women who perpetrate lethal domestic violence, by analyzing the cases of such violence in Houston, Texas, for the period of 1985 to 1999. We first examine intimate partner homicide as a proportion of all Houston homicide over the periods of 1985-1994 and 1996-1999.[1] Then, we disaggregate female intimate partner homicide into three categories by race/ethnicity, as well as the living arrangements of the couple involved. In so doing, our intention is to inform intervention and treatment programs directed toward such women, by noting distinctions in women's involvement as offenders within and among these subgroups.

A NEED FOR INCREASED DIFFERENTIATION AMONG DOMESTIC HOMICIDE OFFENDERS

The debate has been long and volatile regarding the relative levels of domestic violence perpetrated by males and females. When framing recommendations for prevention and treatment of this serious social problem, empirical evidence also suggests that we must differentiate between less serious and more serious forms of domestic hostility. Although some studies consistently argue that there is a high degree of parity in domestic aggression in general, even if males are more likely than females to inflict serious bodily harm to their intimate victims (Straus & Gelles, 1986; Straus, 1990; Stets & Straus, 1990; Morse, 1995). Other researchers insist that such findings are the result of methodological flaws in partner violence assessment and caution of the danger of assuming such parity (Dobash, Dobash, Wilson & Daly, 1992; Saunders, 2002). Still, there is sufficient evidence for the presence of asymmetrical domestic violence (Stets & Straus, 1990; Kwong, Bartholomew & Dutton, 1999) wherein females are the aggressors, that this subgroup should not be ignored. Also, as noted by Kwong et al. (1999), to the degree that we ignore the possibility of women's violence, the credibility of theory and research directed toward ending violence against women is jeopardized. The point here is that both gender and level of aggression are pertinent.

Arguably the motivations for domestic homicide have received the most research attention, with the preponderance of the evidence to date that men are more likely to kill for reasons of retaliation or possessiveness, whereas women do so as a last resort in self-defense (Browne, 1987; Browne, Williams & Dutton, 1999; Langan & Dawson, 1995; Websdale, 1999). While useful, we recognize that this is an oversimplification of the sex-specific etiology of domestic homicide. For example, there was evidence of preplanning by female perpetrators of partner homicide in 27 percent of Jurik and Winn's (1990) cases and in 19.9 percent of cases examined by Coramae Mann (1992). Certainly, some portion of the cases in each instance was a woman taking better thought out approaches to end threats to their own lives. But this is not always the case.

Drawn from the criminological literature is an abundance of evidence that marital status has also proven to be a significant predictor of intimate partner homicide. There is some evidence that men and women in cohabiting relationships, such as common-law marriages or intimates living with each other, are more likely to be killed by their partners than those who are married (Daly & Wilson, 1988; Wilson, Daly & Wright, 1993). For example, in a study conducted in Houston in 1969 (Lundsgaarde, 1977), 40 percent of all female-perpetrated intimate homicides were against cohabiting partners. More recently, Shackleford (2001) found, in his study of more than 400,000 homicides occurring between 1976 and 1994 in the United States, that in cohabiting relationships, men were ten times more likely to be killed by their intimate partner than were married men.

In summary, intimate partner homicide is not simply a dual phenomenon, with aggressive men and defenseless women driven under the worst of interpersonal circumstances to kill one another. To adequately address the issue in both sociological and psychological terms, it must be understood more fully. Given that, between 1985-1999, on average, 723 women killed intimate partners in the U.S. annually (FBI Multiple years), more refined categorization of these women is called for.

The contribution that the present analysis makes to our understanding of women's perpetration of lethal domestic violence is an analysis of intimate partner homicide in Houston for the years 1985-1999. The findings are based on a pre-existing 1985-1994 analysis (Paulsen & Brewer, 2000), coupled with a replication of the analysis for the more recent (1996-1999) time period. Specifically, we disaggregate these homicides by the race/ethnicity of perpetrators, whether the relationship was a registered or *defacto* union and compare women's perpetration of domestic homicide to their commission of all other types of killing.

Sex Ratios of Killing and Spousal Sex Ratios of Killing

The major way that we describe female intimate partner homicide offending in the present study is through a measure known as the sex ratio of killing (SROK). Beginning with the work of Wilson and Daly (1992), the SROK has become a useful measure of women and men's relative involvement as perpetrators of overall, as well as intimate partner (spousal), homicide. This measure is expressed as the ratio of the number of female homicide offenders for every 100 male offenders. Wilson and Daly (1992) analyzed data from six industrialized countries between the years of 1965 and 1989, concluding that the spousal SROK was twice as high in the United States as that of any other country included in their study. According to their findings, for every 100 men in the U.S. who killed their wives, 75 wives killed their husbands.

Wilson and Daly (1992) posited that an explanation for such a discrepancy among the countries was the greater availability of guns, women's increased labor force participation and the tendency for homicide to be less male-based in the United States. Subsequently, Gauthier and Bankston (1997) examined the United States Strokes for the period of 1988 to 1992. They further concluded that the SROK was influenced by economic inequality along with the "traditional cultural orientations to gender roles" (Paulsen & Brewer 2000:90). In Riedel and Best's (1998) analysis of 2,686 intimate partner homicides, disaggregated by relationship, they found that the highest spousal SROKs for each racial and ethnic group occurred among common-law husbands and wives. For African-Americans, the SROK in this category was 132. This indicates that for every 100 male intimate partner homicide offenders there were 132 female offenders; this ratio was twice as high as for any other relationship type among Blacks.

Paulsen and Brewer (2000) took the findings of these researchers a step further in their comparison of the SROKs for intimate partner homicide in Chicago and Houston. Using 1985-1994 data for Houston and 1965-1989 data for Chicago, the researchers found that high SROKs (indicating more parity in female and male offenders) were seen largely among the Black population in both cities, while the lowest SROKs were found among Hispanics. They also concluded that the risk of males being killed by their female partners decreased significantly when the couple was separated.

Recently, Houston's homicide data for the period of 1996-1999 were made available to us. Using the results of the former Houston SROK analysis (Paulsen & Brewer, 2000), for the period of 1985 to 1994, we compare those findings to the final years of the twentieth century. This allows us to note trends in female offending over a longer time period, with the latter being a period in which the incidence of intimate partner homicide was declining nationally (Rosenfeld, 1999).

Our analysis will answer the following questions: (1) What has been the trend in overall and intimate partner homicide in Houston for the 1985-1999 time period? (2) As measured by the sex ratio of killing (SROK), how likely are women to be the offenders in domestic homicide? (3) How does women's lethal violence in domestic incidents vary by race? How does women's lethal violence in domestic incidents vary by whether the relationship is registered or defacto?

DATA AND METHODS

Data for this study were obtained from two sources. The homicide data for both time periods (1985-1994 and 1996-1999)[1] were obtained from computerized files of the Houston Police Department's Homicide Division murder logs. The 1985-1994 data include all deaths that were classified by the HPD as criminal homicides ($N = 4,949$ cases). Intimate partner cases ($n = 334$, 6.7%) were then extracted from the total set for analysis in this study, according to the type of relationship found between the complainant and the suspect. The same was done for the 1996-1999 data, which contained 1,204 total homicide cases, 117 (9.7%) of which were classified as intimate partner homicide. In keeping with police classifications of intimate partner homicide, this study includes husbands/wives, common-law husbands/wives, boyfriends/girlfriends, as well as former/ex-relationships in each of these categories. For 1985-1994, there were also twenty intimate partner homicides classified as homosexual; there were seven such incidents for the 1996-1999 time period. For purposes of computing sex ratios of killing, these cases are excluded from the present analysis.

Population demographics reported herein were taken from U.S. Census data (1993, 2003) for the City of Houston, Texas. In Table 1, selected population characteristics are shown for the years of 1990 and 2000. Houston is one of the most populous cities in the United States, with almost two million residents in the year 2000. The city is diverse in respect to its racial and ethnic makeup, as might be expected of such a large city in close proximity to Mexico. Shown here, as of 2000, Houston has become increasingly Hispanic (37.4%). In this study, we categorize the race and ethnicity of offenders and victims as Black, White (including Asian and Other) and Hispanic.

Definitions

In this analysis, intimate partner homicide is defined as *a killing in which the victim and the offender were current or former spouses, common-law spouses, or dating partners.* Common-law marriages, also known as *defacto* marriages, lack a legal definition, but are usually identified as sexually intimate, cohabiting couples. Each case in this analysis was therefore either classified as a *registered* (marriage) or *defacto* relationship.

As earlier noted, the *sex ratio of killing* (SROK) is defined as the number of female homicide offenders known for every 100 male of-

☐ Table 1: Selected Census Characteristics for Houston, Texas, 1990 and 2000					
	1990		2000		
	Total Number	Percentage	Total Number	Percentage	Net Change 1990-2000
Population	1,630,672	-	1,953,631	-	+ 322,959
Population Density	2,900 per square mile	-	3,372 per square mile	-	+ 472 per square mile
Sex					
Male	808,598	49.6	969,001	49.6	---
Female	822,074	50.4	984,630	50.4	---
Race					
White	860,323	52.8	962,601	49.3	−3.5%
Black	457,574	28.1	494,496	25.3	−3.0%
Other	312,775	19.2	496,525	25.4	+6 %
Ethnicity					
Hispanic	442,943	27.2	730,865	37.4	+10%
Non-Hispanic	1,187,729	72.8	1,222,766	62.6	−10%

fenders in a sample set. For example, if there are 500 known homicide offenders in a certain city for a certain time period, 100 of whom were female and 400 of whom were male, then the SROK would be calculated as $100/400 = 25$. This translates into one female offender for every four male offenders. In turn, the *spousal SROK* represents this ratio for male and female perpetrators of intimate partner homicide. For the SROK portion of our analysis, we analyzed the 4,443 (of 4,949) cases of 1985-1994 Houston homicide and 917 (of 1,207) cases during 1996-1999 for which race/ethnicity and type of relationship (registered or *defacto*) were known.

RESULTS

Question 1: What has been the trend in overall and intimate partner homicide in Houston for the 1985-1999 time period?

We first examine whether overall and intimate partner homicide rates in Houston from the mid-1980s to late-1990s declined, as was true nationally. Results are shown in Table 2. The mean annual homicide rate for 1985-1994 was 28.1, with an average of 44 intimate partner homicides per year (8.9%) for the ten-year period. In the more current time period (1996-1999), there were a total of 1,204 reported homicides, 117 of which were between intimates. The overall homicide rate of 15.4 included an average of 29 (9.7%) incidents involving intimate partners.

These results further indicate that, while the average number of intimate partner homicides per year decreased, the percentage of all homicides that involved intimate partners increased, from 8.9% to 9.7%. One explanation may be found in the total number of homicides during these two time periods. As predicted by Verkko's (1967) static law, the proportion of female victims (who are over-represented in intimate partner homicide) is inversely related to the incidence of homicide in a city. Alternatively, we believe this finding suggests that the circumstances underlying this type of homicide are not as responsive to the forces of economic and criminal justice policy that are thought to predict or explain homicide in general. We note, as well, that during the final year of this analysis, just as overall homicide increased, the proportion of intimate partner homicide decreased by almost 20 percent.

Though not shown, women used guns to commit their domestic homicides in two-thirds of cases for both time periods. In the 1985-1994 period, men used guns two-thirds of the time and in approximately

				Total Intimate Partner Homicides	Mean # Annually	IPH as % of all Homicides
Years	Total Homicides	Mean # Annually	Mean Rate			
1995-1994	4,949	495	28.1	442	44.2	8.9%
1996-1999	1,204	302	15.4	117	29.3	9.7%

□ **Table 2: Overall and Intimate Partner Homicide, Houston, Texas, 1985 to 1999**

one-half of the incidents during the 1996-1999 period. This is in keeping with other studies of weapon use in intimate partner homicide.

Question 2: As measured by the sex ratio of killing (SROK), how likely are women to be offenders in domestic homicide?

The key question in the present study concerns women as the aggressors in intimate partner homicide. Perhaps the most striking initial finding is of the difference in sex ratios of killing when such homicides were between intimate partners, versus those directed toward friends, acquaintances, strangers or other family members. What we found is that in the 1985-1994 period in Houston, 75 women killed intimates per every 100 men who did so. This ratio was ten times greater than that for all other types of homicide, for wherein women were the aggressors in seven cases per every 100 incidents in which men were the perpetrators.

The differential in sex ratios of killing was mirrored in the latter (1996-1999) time period. During this time, the spousal sex ratio of killing was 69, compared to a ration six for other homicide types. This downward trend lends support to the general finding nationally indicating that decreases in intimate partner homicide are actually accruing to a savings of men's lives over those of women (Dugan, Nagin & Rosenfeld, 1999).

These findings for Houston approximate those for the U.S. overall during the 1965-1989 time period of Daly and Wilson's (1992) initial analysis of international spousal sex ratios of killing, wherein the U.S. ratio was 75. Clearly, women's role as the aggressor rivals that of men in this specific category of homicide offending.

Question 3: How does women's lethal violence in domestic incidents vary by race? How does women's lethal violence in domestic incidents vary by whether the relationship is registered or defacto?

Looking at overall SROKs for intimate partners in Table 3, we see a significant difference by racial/ethnic subgroups of couples. For the overall period of this analysis, Blacks have the highest spousal (intimate partner) SROK of the three groups, followed by Whites, then Hispanics. For Blacks, there were actually more women than men killing their intimate partners during the period 1985-1994 and there continued to be near parity within this subgroup for the period 1996-1999. By comparison, 63 White women were the aggressors in intimate partner homicide for every 100 men who were the perpetrators. Notable within Hispanic couples is the doubling of this SROK (24 to 53) in the latter time period. Though based on a small number of cases (68 and 26, respectively), Hispanic women (as a group) were much more likely to be the aggressors in intimate partner homicide during the latter time period.

SROK Among Types of Relationships

Finally, does the form of the relationship matter? In other words, are legally married couples more or less likely to engage in lethal violence than are those who are in *defacto* relationships, including common-law, live-in, boyfriend/girlfriend? In his analysis of intimate partner homicide in St. Louis, Rosenfeld (1997) found that the decrease in intimate partner homicide was a function of the declining rates of marriage. Among female victims of intimate partner homicide, more than 80 percent were killed by their husbands during the period 1968-1972. As of 1988-1992, only 40 percent were killed by their husbands and the others by non-marital intimate partners.

As shown in Table 3, we see that for Blacks, *defacto* relationships had higher intimate partner SROKS in both time periods. For 1996-1999, 94 women per 100 men were the homicide offenders in defacto relationships, compared to 80 women per 100 men in married couples. There appears to be a protective advantage to men in married couple relationships not afforded to common-law or other intimate partners. This was also the case for Whites in the 1996-1999 period, in which there were 79 female aggressors per 100 male aggressors in defacto relationships, compared to 46 women per 100 men in married couple intimate partner homicides. This is in keeping with Riedel and Best's (1998) study of intimate homicides in California, where they

□ **Table 3: Overall and Spousal/Intimate Partner Sex Ratios of Killing (SROKs) by Race/Ethnicity and Relationship Type, Houston, TX, 1985-1999**

Relationship Type	1985-94 Offender				1996-99 Offender			
Intimate Partners	Man (#/%)	Woman (#/%)	Total (#/%)	SROK	Man (#/%)	Woman (#/%)	Total (#/%)	SROK
All Other Homicide	251 (56.8)	191 (43.2)	442 (100)	76	65 (59.0)	45 (41.0)	110 (100)	69
SROKs by Race/Ethnicity & Relationship Type*	3,757 (93.9)	244 (6.1)	4001 (100)	7	763 (94.5)	44 (5.5)	807 (100)	6
Black								
All Intimate Partners	130 (49.6)	132 (50.4)	262 (100)	102	21 (52.5)	19 (47.5)	40 (100)	91
Registered	43 (56.6)	33 (43.4)	76	77	5 (55.6)	4 (44.4)	9	80
defacto	87 (46.8)	99 (53.2)	186	114	16 (51.6)	15 (48.4)	31	94
All Other Homicides	1,898 (91.8)	170 (8.2)	2,068 (100)	9	319 (95.2)	16 (4.8)	335 (100)	5
White, Asian, Other								
All Intimate Partners	60 (61.2)	38 (38.8)	98 (100)	63	27 (61.4)	17 (38.6)	44 (100)	63
Registered	40 (57.1)	30 (42.9)	70	75	13 (68.4)	6 (31.6)	19	46
defacto	20 (71.4)	8 (28.6)	28	40	14 (56.0)	11 (44.0)	25	79
All Other Homicides	572 (92.1)	49 (7.9)	621 (100)	9	235 (95.9)	10 (4.1)	245 (100)	4
Hispanic								
All Intimate Partners	55 (80.9)	13 (19.1)	68 (100)	24	17 (65.4)	9 (34.6)	26 (100)	53
Registered	20 (71.4)	8 (28.6)	28	40	6 (60.0)	4 (40.0)	10	67
defacto	35 (87.5)	5 (12.5)	40	14	11 (68.8)	5 (31.2)	16	45
All Other Homicides	1,183 (98.0)	24 (2.0)	1,207 (100)	2	209 (92.1)	18 (7.9)	227 (100)	9

* Results for 4,443 (1985-1994) and 917 (1996-1999) known race/ethnicity and relationship type of offenders.
Excludes 20 (1985-1994) and 7 (1996-1999) homosexual relationships.

found that the highest SROKs were exhibited among common-law couples.

Among Hispanics, though the raw numbers of incidents of intimate partner homicide in defacto relationships were larger than those for married couples over the 1985-1999 time span, Hispanic women were the perpetrators in a larger proportion of married couple cases in both time periods. Our speculation for this difference by race/ethnicity may be a function of more traditional family forms among Hispanics that (1) may place pressure on women to remain in otherwise unacceptable marriages and (2) discourages non-marital unions.

CONCLUSION

Women as the aggressors in intimate partner homicide were the primary focus of the present study. Our findings suggest that, as has been true nationally, there has been a stronger downward trend in men's rates of homicide victimization at the hands of intimate partners than has been true for women. Yet a more precise picture emerges when these spousal sex ratios of killing are disaggregated by race/ethnicity.

As in the original 1985-1994 Houston study (Paulsen & Brewer, 2000), the spousal SROKs continue to be near parity for Blacks. Specifically, during the 1996-1999 period, for every 100 Black men who killed their intimate partners, there were 90 Black women who were the perpetrators of this lethal violence. For both time periods, 63 White (including Asian/Other) women killed their domestic partners, per 100 White men who committed such acts. From small numbers of cases for each time period, Hispanic women's spousal/intimate partner SROK doubled in the latter time period. Between 1996 and 1999, 53 Hispanic women were the assailants in intimate partner homicide per 100 Hispanic men who were the perpetrators. Regarding the form of these unions, results of this analysis of Houston intimate partner homicide indicated that between both Black and White subgroups of couples, women were a larger proportion of the assailants in defacto (i.e., common-law, girlfriend/boyfriend) relationships than in married couples.

As earlier suggested, these disparities by racial/ethnic subgroup are open to interpretation. In cases of women who kill intimate partners, self-defense continues to be recognized as the most frequent explanation for women resorting to lethal violence. Yet there may be other plausible explanations for such violence, based upon the racial/ethnic subgroup to which these women belong, and the attendant cultural and motivational differences among them. For example, the dynamics of lethal violence for Black couples often have less patriarchal underpinnings than those of Hispanic couples. In turn, anecdotal evidence suggests that Black women may consider calls for police assistance in domestic violence disputes to be futile, thereby leading to the decision to take matters into their own hands. Coming from traditionally more patriarchal family systems, Hispanic women are often conditioned to be more fearful of retribution by their male partners. In either case, police awareness of significant differences in the likelihood of such altercations becoming fatal may serve to reduce the number of such fatalities.

Though we do not yet have sufficient information regarding the socioeconomic backgrounds or criminal histories of the female intimate partner homicide offenders in these data, our findings do highlight the importance of taking the subcultures from which these offenders come into account when devising correctional intervention strategies. Interventions for women who commit self-defensive non-lethal and lethal assault may prove ineffective for women who, for reasons still to be refined, are more violence-prone in general, a manifestation of which may be domestic violence/homicide.

As noted by Kwong et al. (1999), it is important that we continue research that enhances our understanding of all forms of violence within intimate relationships, thereby guiding our efforts to develop appropriate preventative and therapeutic approaches. Those researchers rightly argue that it is imperative that clinicians be open to a range of abuse patterns that differ in frequency, severity, and direction. Psychological assessments of incarcerated women who kill their husbands, modeled after those for incarcerated men who kill their wives (Biro, Puccini & Djuric, 1992; Dutton & Kerry, 1999), are called for.

The lessons being increasingly learned about interventions with offenders in non-lethal domestic violence may be instructive for interventions with those who have killed their partners. From his review of research on domestic violence and batterer intervention programs, Saunders (2002) makes the point that firm conclusions about best practices are premature because the programs that presently exist have not been well evaluated. Based on the increasing evidence of variability among domestically violent men, he concluded that multiple forms of intervention are needed to be able to respond to motivational and cultural differences among abusers.

NOTE

1. In the mid-1990s, the Houston Police Department underwent a major change in internal data collection and analysis. For this reason, 1995 data was inadvertently unavailable.

REFERENCES

Browne, A. (1987) *When Battered Women Kill*. New: Free Press.

Browne, A. & Williams, K. (1993). Gender, intimacy, and lethal violence: Trends from 1976 through 1987. *Gender and Society, 7*, 78-98.

Browne, A., Williams, K., & Dutton, D.G. (1999). Homicide between intimate partners: a 20-year review. In M.D. Smith and M. Zahn (eds.), *Homicide: A Sourcebook of Social Research*. Thousand Oaks, CA: Sage.

Daly, M. & Wilson, M. (1988). *Homicide*. Hawthorne, NY; Aldine.

Dobash R.P., Dobash R.E., Wilson, M., & Daly, M. (1992). The myth of sexual symmetry in marital violence. *Social Problems, 39*(1), 71-91.

Dugan, L., Nagin, D., & Rosenfeld, R. (1999). Explaining the decline in intimate partner homicide: The effects of changing domesticity, women's status, and domestic violence resources. *Homicide Studies, 3*, 187-214.

Dutton, D.G. & Kerry, G. (1999). Personality profiles and modi operandi of spousal homicide perpetrators. *International Journal of Law & Psychiatry, 22*(3-4), 287-300.

Durkheim, E. (1897/1951). *Suicide: A Study of Sociology*. Trans. George Simpson. Glencoe, IL: The Free Press.

Federal Bureau of Investigation. (2003). *Supplementary Homicide Reports, 1976-2002*. Retrieved January 20, 2005, from U.S. Department of Justice, Bureau of Justice Statistics Web site: http://www.ojp.usdoj.gov/bjs/homicide/tables/intimatestab.htm.

Gauthier, D. & Bankston, W. (1997). Gender equality and the sex ratio of intimate killing. *Criminology, 35*, 577-600.

Greenfeld, L., Rand, M., Craven, D., Klaus, P., Perkins, C., Ringel, C., Warchol, G., Maston, C., & Fox, J. (1998). *Violence by Intimates*. Washington, DC: U.S. Department of Justice.

Jurik, N. & Winn, R. (1990). Gender and homicide: A comparison of men and women who kill. *Violence and Victims, 5*, 227-242.

Kwong, M.J., Bartholomew, K., & Dutton, D.G. (1999). Gender differences in patterns of relationship violence in Alberta. *Canadian Journal of Behavioural Science*, 008400X, July 1, Vol. 31, Issue 3.

Langan, P. & Dawson, J. (1995). Spouse murder defendants in large urban counties. Washington, DC: U.S. Department of Justice, Bureau of Justice Statistics. NCJ 153256.

Leonard, E.D. (2002). *Convicted Survivors: The Imprisonment of Battered Women Who Kill*. New York: State University Press.

Lundsgaarde, H.P. (1977). *Murder in Space City*. New York: Oxford.

Makepeace, J. (1997). Courtship violence as process: A developmental theory. In A. Cardelli (ed.), *Violence Between Intimate Partners: Patterns, Causes, and Effects.* (pp. 29-47). Boston: Allyn & Bacon.

Mann, C.R. (1992). Female murderers and their motives: a tale of two cities. In E. Viano (ed.), *Intimate Violence: Interdisciplinary Perspectives.* Bristol, PA: Taylor and Francis.

Mercy, J. & Saltzman, L. (1989). Fatal violence among spouses in the United States, 1976-1985. *American Journal of Public Health, 79,* 595-599.

Morse, B.J. (1995). Beyond the conflict tactics scale: Assessing gender differences in partner violence. *Violence and Victims, 10,* 251-272.

Paulsen, D. & Brewer V. (2000). The spousal SROK revisited: A comparison of Chicago and Houston intimate partner homicide ratios. *Gender Issues, 18,* 88-100.

Riedel, M. & Best, J. (1998). Patterns in intimate partner homicide: California, 1987-1996. *Homicide Studies, 2,* 305-320.

Riedel, M. & Lewitt, K. (1998). Homicide in Los Angeles County: A study of racial and ethnic victimization. Unpublished manuscript. As cited in Riedel & Best (1998), *Patterns in intimate partner homicide: California, 1987-1996.*

Rosenfeld, R. (1997). Changing relationships between men and women: A note on the decline in intimate partner homicide. *Homicide Studies, 1,* 72-83.

Saunders, D.G. (2002). Are physical assaults by wives and girlfriends a major social problem: A review of the literature. *Violence Against Women, 8*(12), 1424-1448.

Shackelford, T. (2001). Partner-killing by women in cohabiting relationships and marital relationships. *Homicide Studies, 5,* 253-266.

Stets, J.E. & Straus, M.A. (1990). Gender differences in reporting marital violence and its medical and psychological consequences. In M.A. Straus & R.J. Gelles (eds.), *Physical Violence n American Families: Risk Factors and Adaptations to Violence in 8,145 Families.* New Brunswick, NJ: Transaction Publishing: 227-244.

Straus, M.A. (1990). Injury and frequency of assault and the "representative sample fallacy" in measuring wife beating and child abuse. In M.A. Straus & & R.J. Gelles (eds.), *Physical Violence in American Families: Risk Factors and Adaptations to Violence in 8,145 Families.* New Brunswick, NJ: Transaction Publishing: 75-91.

Straus, M.A. & Gelles, R.J. (1986). Society change and change in family violence from 1975 to 1985 as revealed by two national surveys. *Journal of Marriage and the Family, 48,* 465-479.

U.S. Bureau of the Census. 1993, 2003: *Population and Housing Characteristics.* Washington, DC: U.S. Government Printing Office.

Verkko, V. (1967). Static and dynamic "laws" of sex and homicide. In M. Wolfgang (Ed.), *Studies in Homicide.* New York: Harper & Row, 36-44.

Websdale, N. (1999). *Understanding Domestic Homicide.* Boston: Northeastern University Press.

Wilson, M. & Daly, M. (1992). Who kills whom in spousal killings? On the exceptional sex ratio of spousal homicides in the United States. *Criminology, 30,* 189-211.

Wilson, M., Daly, M., & Wright, C. (1993). Uxoricide in Canada: Demographic risk patterns. *Canadian Journal of Criminology, 35,* 263-291.

AUTHORS' NOTES

Victoria B. Titterington, PhD, is Associate Professor in the College of Criminal Justice of Sam Houston State University. Her research interests include lethal and non-lethal family violence and correctional issues, as well as aging and crime.

Laura Harper was, at this writing, a correctional officer with the Texas Department of Criminal Justice. She completed her graduate work in the College of Criminal Justice of Sam Houston State University, with a thesis entitled "Law Enforcement Response to Reports of Stalking in the United States." Her areas of interest are domestic violence and stalking.

The authors would like to acknowledge Capt. Richard Holland of the Homicide Division of the Houston Police Department for his provision of the homicide data necessary for this analysis as well as his ongoing support of Houston-related homicide research.

Address correspondence to Dr. Victoria Titterington, College of Criminal Justice, P.O. Box 2296, Sam Houston State University, Huntsville, TX 77341-2296 (E-mail: icc_vbt@shsu.edu).

Women Who Perpetrate Relationship Violence: Moving Beyond Political Correctness. Pp. 99-124.

Available online at http://www.haworthpress.com/web/JOR

© 2005 by The Haworth Press, Inc. All rights reserved.

doi:10.1300/J076v41n04_05

Investigating Intersections Between Gender and Intimate Partner Violence Recidivism

BRIAN RENAUER
KRIS HENNING

ABSTRACT Mandatory and preferred arrest policies for domestic violence (DV) have led to an increase in DV arrests and prosecutions of male and female suspects. The strain of this increase on criminal justice resources suggests a need for prioritizing DV cases and determining suspects most at risk for recidivism and victimization. The present study sought to address a largely ignored question in the field of DV: who is more likely to recidivate, male or female DV offenders involved with the criminal justice system? Two forms of recidivism were coded using subsequent police reports for DV: recidivism as a suspect and recidivism as a victim. The results indicate that there are significant differences in the ways in which male and female DV offenders recidivate. Males were more likely to recidivate as a suspect and females were more likely to be listed as a future DV victim in police reports. Male and female offenders also significantly differed in the frequency of their recidivism. Gender, independent of other factors, was reliably associated with both forms of recidivism and a similar pattern of recidivism was found in two different cities. There was, however, a small group of female offenders in both cities who appear to be primary aggressors. Another grouping of female offenders appears to be involved in relationships characterized by mutual aggression and bi-directional violence.

Together these two groups account for roughly a quarter of the women in our sample. The implications of the findings for arrest practices, treatment and interventions, and using gender as a risk factor are discussed. Validity and reliability problems with using police reports as a measure of DV recidivism are also reviewed. *[Article copies available for a fee from The Haworth Document Delivery Service: 1-800-HAWORTH. E-mail address: <docdelivery@ haworthpress.com> Website: <http://www.HaworthPress.com> © 2005 by The Haworth Press, Inc. All rights reserved.]*

KEYWORDS Domestic violence, gender differences, recidivism, female batterers

GENDER AND INTIMATE PARTNER VIOLENCE RECIDIVISM

Over the past thirty years the combined forces of research, victim advocacy, and litigation have changed public policy regarding domestic violence (DV) from a neglected "family problem" to a problem of significant concern for most criminal justice agencies (Fagan, 1996). Perhaps the most obvious change has been in law enforcement. Jurisdictions across the country have passed legislation that either encourages or requires police make an arrest when an assault has occurred between intimate partners (Miller, 1998; Sherman & Cohn, 1989). As might be expected, these laws have led to dramatic increases in the number of suspects taken into police custody (Mignon & Holmes, 1995; Victim Services Agency, 1989). Prosecutors also have changed their practices for dealing with DV in recent years. Whereas previously fewer than 10% of detained suspects were charged (e.g., Ford, 1993; Rauma, 1984; Schmidt & Steury, 1989; Sherman, 1992), prosecutors in some jurisdictions now pursue charges against the majority of defendants (Henning & Feder, in press). These two factors, increased arrests and prosecution, have resulted in significant strains on agencies interacting with DV offenders (e.g., police, pretrial services, prosecutors, judges, public defenders, probation). Moreover, many of these agencies have been forced to manage this increased caseload with fewer and fewer resources. As a result, criminal justice agencies are increasingly confronted with the task of prioritizing cases; they must identify certain DV cases that require an intensive response while others receive secondary attention or no intervention at all (Kropp, 2004; Roehl & Guertin, 2000).

Historically, criminal justice professionals relied on informal procedures to identify DV cases they believed were worthy of further attention. For example, early research on policing practices identified a host of factors related to officers' decision to arrest a DV suspect as opposed to issuing a warning or temporarily separating those involved. This included the suspect's prior criminal record, the suspect's use of drugs or alcohol, the presence of a weapon, and victim injuries. All of these factors increased the likelihood that officers made an arrest of the suspect (Eigenberg, Scaborough, & Kappeler, 1996; Ferraro, 1989; Smith, 1987; Smith & Klein, 1984). Similarly, prosecutors appeared more likely to pursue a case when it involved a "good victim" (e.g., cooperative, injured during attack, not arrested) and a "bad offender" (e.g., intoxicated, prior criminal arrests, used weapon, injured victim; Henning & Feder, in press; Rauma, 1984).

While consideration of the victim's injuries, the use of a weapon, and a cooperative victim certainly makes sense from an evidentiary perspective, there may have been another motivation for informally considering such factors when deciding which cases to fully pursue. Specifically, police and prosecutors are often concerned with the potential for future assaults against victims (e.g., Kane, 2000). This is particularly true in the case of DV involving intimate partners, where the ongoing relationship between most victims and offenders increases the likelihood of further conflicts. Recidivism rates ranging from 28 to 40% have been reported among male spouse abusers (Gondolf, 1997; Grann & Wedin, 2002; Maxwell, Garner, & Fagan, 2001) and the majority of men who kill their spouse/partner have previously been identified by the criminal justice system as batterers (Aldridge & Browne, 2003; Moracco, Runyan, & Butts, 1998). Thus, it is no surprise that criminal justice agencies have sought more formalized methods for prioritizing DV cases based on suspects' risk for recidivism and lethal assaults (Roehl & Guertin, 2000). Such efforts fit into the broader role being taken by various legal institutions to protect DV victims and hold offenders accountable for their actions (Fagan, 1996).

Domestic Violence, Recidivism, and Risk Assessment

This increased attention on DV recidivism and victim protection has led to the development of numerous risk assessment measures and scales. Among others this includes the Danger Assessment Scale (DAS; Campbell, 1995), the Kingston Screening Instrument for Domestic Violence (K-SID; Gelles & Tolman, 1998), the Ontario Domestic Assault Risk Assessment (ODARA; Hilton, Harris, Rice, Lang, & Cormier, 2004), and the Spousal Assault Risk Assessment (SARA; Kropp, Hart, Webster, & Eaves, 1998). The development of risk scales typically involves several stages. Potential risk factors for DV recidivism are identified using either the research literature or clinical experience. Common risk factors include such things as the offender's abuse of substances, exposure to violence in childhood, personality disorder, attitudes that support the use of violence, severe jealousy, assaults of non-family members, and prior DV offenses (Saunders, 1995; Dutton & Kropp, 2000). These individual items are then combined into a larger measure that is completed by the victim, an advocate, a criminal justice professional, or a mental health provider.

In theory at least, structured risk assessments and actuarial scales are more accurate in predicting recidivism than informal judgments made by criminal justice and mental health professionals (Grove & Meehl, 1996; Quinsey, Harris, Rice, & Cormier, 1998). With but a few exceptions, however (e.g., DAS: Campbell et al., 2003; ODARA: Hilton et al., 2004; SARA: Kropp et al., 1998), most of the scales currently available to assess risk for DV recidivism have not been sufficiently validated to warrant this degree of confidence. More importantly for the present study is the fact that none of the DV risk scales currently described in the literature consider gender as a potential risk factor. In every case the scales were specifically developed for, and in rare cases validated with, male offenders who have assaulted a female intimate partner.

Gender and Domestic Violence

Gender is an increasingly important issue to police, prosecutors, and other criminal justice professionals because both the number and proportion of DV arrests that involve females have risen as a result of mandatory/preferred arrest laws (Chesney-Lind, 2002; Miller, 2001). It is more common now for officers responding to domestic disputes to arrest both members of the couple (e.g., dual arrest) when they cannot quickly determine who is primarily responsible for the offense (Hirschel & Buzawa, 2002; Martin, 1997; Miller, 2001). Other women are being singly arrested when officers identify them as the primary aggressor. It is not unusual, therefore, for women to account for as much as one quarter of the DV arrests in a given jurisdiction (Henning & Feder, 2004; Martin, 1997; Miller, 2001; Swan & Snow, 2002).

This rise in women arrested for intimate partner violence in particular worries many of those who originally supported mandatory arrest laws as a means of protecting women (Chesney-Lind, 2002; McMahon & Pence, 2003). Of greatest concern is the possibility that most of the women arrested are victims of abuse who simply chose to defend themselves during an attack by their spouse/partner (Hamberger & Potente, 1994; Miller, 2001; Saunders, 1995). Once arrested, these victims may be less willing to seek assistance from the criminal justice system (Crager, Cousin, & Hardy, 2003). Hirschel and Buzawa (2002) have described other negative consequences that may result from abused women being arrested, including the loss of services designated for victims, financial and employment problems, and child custody difficulties.

McMahon and Pence (2003) have offered several suggestions for addressing these concerns regarding women arrested for DV. First, they argue that law enforcement officers need additional training to differentiate offensive aggression versus acts committed in self-defense. Second, officers should be instructed or mandated by law to arrest only the primary aggressor from an incident. To do this McMahon and Pence (2003) recommend that officers consider who would be at greatest risk if no arrest were made. Third, they suggest that advocates work with attorneys to more aggressively defend women charged with DV. Fourth, advocates should discourage prosecutors from pursuing charges against female DV arrestees. Finally, in the rare cases where women are convicted of DV they should not be ordered to attend offender-oriented programs. Instead, they should participate in groups that offer instruction regarding the law (i.e., appropriate use of self-defense), that discuss their attachment to an abusive spouse/partner, and that help the women navigate through various social service agencies that might provide them assistance.

An underlying assumption made by McMahon and Pence (2003) and others writing on this issue (e.g., Chesney-Lind, 2002; Miller, 2001; Saunders, 1995) is that women who are arrested for intimate partner violence pose little threat to their spouse/partner. This may in part explain the greater leniency shown to female defendants who are arrested for DV against a male intimate (Henning & Renauer, in press). Whether women are less likely to recidivate than men has not been sufficiently addressed using empirical procedures.

This leads to the central question posed by the present study: Who is more likely to recidivate, male or female DV offenders?[1] Providing an answer to this question could give police, prosecutors and others a legitimate justification for granting female DV offenders greater leniency than men. Alternatively, the findings could highlight a need for greater control over female DV perpetrators and the expansion of victim services to their male intimate partners. Research addressing the relationship between gender and recidivism could also contribute to the debate on the equivalency of intimate partner violence between men and women. Some family violence researchers and men's advocacy groups have argued that women are just as likely to use physical aggression in intimate relationships as men and that greater attention needs to be given to female perpetrators (e.g., Archer, 2000; McNeely, Cook, & Torres, 2001; Straus, 2005). Those who argue that DV is a gendered crime point to contradictory data showing that male offenders and female victims are overrepresented in clinical samples (e.g., homicide statistics, shelters, emergency rooms, crime surveys; Cascardi & Vivian, 1995; Loseke & Kurz, 2005; Tjaden & Thoennes, 2000) and they critique the methodologies used by researchers finding equal rates of aggression between men and women (Saunders, 2002). Lastly, research on gender and recidivism should inform us as to whether gender should be considered as a risk factor when evaluating DV offenders and developing risk assessment scales.

After carefully reviewing the literature only one published study was found that examined gender as a potential predictor of DV recidivism. Wooldredge and Thistlethwaite (2002) used a sample containing 3,110 adults (84% male; 16% female) arrested for misdemeanor assault against an intimate partner. Gender was entered as one of several predictor variables in a multivariate logistic regression equation predicting re-arrest for misdemeanor or felony intimate assault during a two-year follow up. They found that males were significantly more likely than females to be rearrested. Studies of recidivism among general offenders (i.e., all types of offenses) reveal a similar pattern: female offenders are less likely to recidivate than male offenders (Gendreau, Little, & Goggin, 1996; Jones & Sims, 1997; Langan & Levin, 2002) and women tend to be more compliant on probation than men (Olson, Alderden, & Lurigio, 2003).

In the present study we sought to further evaluate whether female DV offenders are less likely to recidivate than their male counterparts. In addition, we sought to test the assumption that many of the women arrested for DV are really victims (e.g., Chesney-Lind, 2002; McMahon

& Pence, 2003; Miller, 2001; Saunders, 1995). To do this we used two data sets that each draw upon a unique sample of male and female DV cases. Two forms of recidivism were coded using subsequent police reports for DV: recidivism as a suspect and recidivism as a victim. Based on prior research, we expected that male offenders would recidivate as suspects at higher rates than female offenders. If not, then female DV offenders pose an equal threat to their spouse/partner. Conversely, we expected that female offenders would be more likely than males to show up in later police reports as the victim of a new DV offense. This difference in future victimization may be an indication that many female offenders were victims who acted in self defense in the incident that caused their original arrest.

METHODS

Databases containing information on DV suspects were obtained from police departments in two cities: Memphis, TN, and Portland, OR. The sample and procedures used for each dataset are described below.

Memphis

Participants. The Memphis sample consisted of 880 suspects (440 men, 440 women) identified in local police reports as having committed a DV offense against a current or former heterosexual intimate partner in 1997. The mean age of the suspects was 31.6 ($SD = 8.7$) and the majority were African-American (75.6%) or Caucasian (23.4%). More of the suspects were (or had been) dating the victim from their instant offense (53.3%) as opposed to being currently/formerly married (46.7%).

Procedure. Cases for inclusion in the sample were selected in the following manner. Using the entire database of DV offense reports for 1997 we identified all of the suspects who had committed an offense against a current/former heterosexual intimate partner. Suspects were included regardless of whether they had been arrested or not.[2] We then eliminated cases where the suspect's full name and date of birth were not recorded: these variables were required to track the suspects over time. This process resulted in the identification of 460 female and 4,882 male suspects. Another 20 records for the women represented repeat offenses as a suspect within the same year. Only the first record was retained for each of these women, leaving us with a total of 440 female suspects meeting the above criteria. A random sample of 440 male suspects was taken from the larger pool of 4,882 for comparison to the women. Duplicate records representing repeat offenses were replaced with randomly selected cases where necessary.

Variables. Several demographic variables were available to describe the sample, including the age of the suspects, their race/ethnicity, the victim-offender relationship, and of course gender. Recidivism information was obtained using a database that contained all DV reports for the region from January 1997 through December 2002, yielding a minimum follow-up time of five years. For each of the 880 suspects we searched for DV reports subsequent to their instant offense. Once again, it did not matter whether the individual was arrested or not, so long as they were listed in a later report. Matches were determined using the individual's name, date of birth, and by reviewing the narrative of each new offense. Two specific forms of recidivism were coded. First, we identified the total number of new reports in which the participant was listed as a *suspect*. Second, we counted the number of times the given individual showed up as a *victim* in subsequent reports.

Portland

Participants. The Portland sample consisted of 6,010 individuals (5,289 men, 721 women) who were identified in city police reports as a suspect in a DV offense from the year 2000. The mean age of the suspects was 34.2 (*SD* = 10.0). The majority of participants were Caucasian (62.3%), followed by African-American (24.6%), Hispanic (8.4%) and other racial/ethic backgrounds (4.8%).

Procedure. DV data for the city of Portland were obtained from the Portland Police Bureau. The database they provided contained identifying information on all suspects and victims involved in crimes that occurred between intimate partners or family members in the year 2000. The initial list of 12,036 named suspects was pared down to 8,706 unique cases, leaving only the first record for each person when multiple records were found (i.e., they recidivated in the same year). In contrast to the records from Memphis, the Portland database did not consistently record the nature of the relationship between suspects and victims. This made it impossible to select only DV cases involving heterosexual intimate partners. Several steps were taken to insure that the majority of cases in the final sample met this criterion. First, all records listing multiple suspects (*n* = 845) and/or multiple victims (*n* = 809) were eliminated. Second, cases with suspects and/or victims under the age of 18 were removed on the belief that some of these involved parent-child incidents or conflicts between siblings ($n = 599$). Finally, 443 cases were removed because the victim and offender were of the same gender. This resulted in a final sample size of 6,010 suspects, including 5,289 men (88%) and 721 women (12%). Consistent with the procedures used in Memphis, suspects were included in the final sample regardless of whether they had been arrested or not.

Variables. Only three demographic variables were available to describe the Portland sample: the suspect's age at the time of the instant offense, his/her race or ethnicity, and gender. Recidivism information was coded using a database of all DV offenses in the city that were reported between January 2000 and December 2003. In contrast to Memphis, the Portland Police Bureau's database contained a unique ID code for each suspect. Data entry clerks are trained to do a comprehensive search of historical records prior to generating new ID codes for people listed in offense reports. This allowed us to use each suspects' unique ID code to identify new DV offenses that came after his/her instant offense. Once again, it did not matter whether the individual was arrested or not, so long as they were listed in a later report. Nor did the later offense have to involve the same victim. This process resulted in the creation of two variables that are consistent with the data coded in Memphis: the total number of new reports in which the participant was listed as a *suspect*, and the number of times the given individual showed up as a *victim* in subsequent reports.

Analysis

The Pearson Chi-Square statistic is used in all the analyses to measure the association between the two nominal variables of interest; gender (female or male) and recidivism (yes or no). A Chi-Square probability of .05 or less was used to reject the null hypothesis that gender is unrelated (that is, only randomly related) to recidivism. Logistic regression models were also used to assess the independent association between gender and recidivism. The logistic regression models are only used to confirm whether significant gender differences in DV recidivism and victimization remain when controlling for demographic differences. These models are not used to test a prediction model of recidivism, which would ideally involve much more information on the suspects and victims not available to us (i.e., Danger Assessment Scale, offense history, drug abuse, etc.).

RESULTS

Table 1 begins by showing some of the demographic characteristics of the male and female offenders in the Memphis sample. The males in the sample were significantly older than the females at the time of their instant offense (F = 9.01, df = 1, $p < .01$) and they differed in the type of

☐ **Table 1: Recidivism Rates of Male and Female Domestic Violence Offenders in Memphis, TN**			
	Suspect Gender		
Demographics & Recidivism Information	Male ($n = 440$)	Female ($n = 440$)	F or χ^2
Age at Instant Offense (SD)	32.5 (9.2)	30.7 (8.1)	9.01**
Race/Ethnicity			4.3
African-American (n)	78.4 (345)	72.7 (320)	
Caucasian (n)	20.5 (90)	26.4 (116)	
Other (n)	1.1 (5)	.9 (4)	
Victim-Offender Relationship			11.9***
Current/Former Dating Partner (n)	59.1 (260)	47.5 (209)	
Spouse/Ex-Spouse (n)	40.9 (180)	52.5 (231)	
DV Recidivism–Any New Report			.1
No Recidivism (n)	56.8 (250)	55.9 (246)	
Recidivism as Suspect or Victim (n)	43.2 (190)	44.1 (194)	
DV Recidivism–Type of Involvement			160.7***
No Recidivism (n)	56.8 (250)	55.9 (246)	
Recidivism as Suspect Only (n)	31.1 (137)	6.1 (27)	
Recidivism as Victim Only (n)	2.5 (11)	26.1 (115)	
Recidivism as Suspect and Victim (n)	9.5 (42)	11.8 (52)	
Repeat DV Recidivism as Suspect			62.4***
No Recidivism (n)	59.3 (261)	82.0 (361)	
One Incident (n)	21.8 (96)	13.2 (58)	
Two or More Incidents (n)	18.9 (83)	4.8 (21)	
Repeat DV Recidivism as Victim			89.1***
No Recidivism (n)	88.0 (387)	62.0 (273)	
One Incident (n)	10.2 (45)	21.4 (94)	
Two or More Incidents (n)	1.8 (8)	16.6 (73)	
*p < .05 **p < .01 ***p < .001			

relationship they had with their alleged victim: the men more commonly offended against a current/former dating partner, whereas the women were more likely to be involved with a spouse/ex-spouse (χ^2 = 11.9, df = 1, p < .001). No racial differences were observed across gender (χ^2 = 4.3, df = 2, p = .115). In both cases the majority of the offenders were African-American.

Table 1 also provides the results of analyses on the relationship between gender and recidivism. The first comparison tested whether male and female offenders differed in their likelihood of showing up in later DV reports, either as a victim or a suspect (i.e., any involvement). The resulting cross-tabulation and Chi-square statistic suggested that there was no gender difference: 43% of the men and 44% of the women had some type of involvement in later police reports involving a domestic offense (χ^2 = .1, df = 1, p = .786). A second analysis explored the types of involvement that the men and women had in these subsequent offenses. Each offender was classified as either a suspect-only recidivist, a victim-only recidivist, a combined recidivist (i.e., reports listing him/her as suspect and victim in different offenses), or a non-recidivist. The 2 × 4 cross-tabulation yielded a significant overall Chi-square (χ^2 = 160.7, df = 3, p < .001), suggesting that male and female DV offenders recidivate in different ways. Specifically, males were much more likely to recidivate as suspects-only (31% vs. 6%), whereas females were more likely to recidivate as victims-only (26% vs. 3%). A smaller percentage of male (10%) and female (12%) offenders appeared as both a suspect and a victim in future incidents. Additional analyses determined whether male and female offenders exhibited differences in the frequency of their recidivism. Men were more likely to be a repeat recidivist as a suspect (19% vs. 5% with 2+ new offenses) (χ^2 = 62.4, df = 2, p < .001). Women were more likely to have multiple offense reports listing them as a victim (17% vs. 2%) (χ^2 = 89.1, df = 2, p < .001). Although male DV offenders appear more often as future suspects, a small percentage of the female offenders (6%) did recidivate as suspects only, some were repeat suspects, and a larger percentage were both a future suspect and victim (12%).

Table 2 presents the demographic and recidivism data from Portland. As a group, the male offenders in the sample were older than the females (F = 30.3, df = 1, p < .001). There were also significant racial differences, with the male offenders being more racially/ethnically diverse than the females (χ^2 = 44.1, df = 3, p < .001). The recidivism data for Portland revealed an identical pattern of findings as those obtained us-

	Suspect Gender		
	Male	Female	
Demographics & Recidivism Information	(n = 5,289)	(n = 721)	F or χ^2
Age at Instant Offense (SD)	34.3 (10.1)	32.1 (9.6)	30.3***
Race/Ethnicity			44.1***
African-American (n)	24.9 (1319)	22.1 (159)	
Caucasian (n)	61.3 (3244)	69.1 (498)	
Hispanic (n)	9.2 (484)	2.6 (19)	
Other (n)	4.6 (242)	6.2 (45)	
DV Recidivism–Any New Report			1.4
No Recidivism (n)	52.1 (2758)	49.8 (359)	
Recidivism as Suspect or Victim (n)	47.9 (2531)	50.2 (362)	
DV Recidivism–Type of Involvement			969.9***
No Recidivism (n)	52.1 (2758)	49.8 (359)	
Recidivism as Suspect Only (n)	38.9 (2059)	8.3 (60)	
Recidivism as Victim Only (n)	1.9 (100)	25.0 (180)	
Recidivism as Suspect and Victim (n)	7.0 (372)	16.9 (122)	
Repeat DV Recidivism as Suspect			119.3***
No Recidivism (n)	54.0 (2858)	74.8 (539)	
One Incident (n)	19.8 (1046)	14.4 (104)	
Two or More Incidents (n)	26.2 (1385)	10.8 (78)	
Repeat DV Recidivism as Victim			815.1***
No Recidivism (n)	91.1 (4817)	58.1 (419)	
One Incident (n)	6.6 (348)	16.6 (120)	
Two or More Incidents (n)	2.3 (124)	25.2 (182)	

☐ **Table 2: Recidivism Rates of Male and Female Domestic Violence Offenders in Portland, OR**

*p < .05 **p < .01 ***p < .001

ing the Memphis sample. Male (52%) and female offenders (50%) were equally likely to appear in subsequent DV police reports (i.e., any involvement) (χ^2 = 1.4, df = 1, p = .235). Like Memphis, however, the type of involvement that male and female offenders had in later DV incidents differed (χ^2 = 969.9, df = 3, p < .001). Male offenders were significantly more likely to recidivate as suspects-only (39% vs. 8%), while females were more likely to recidivate as victims-only (25% vs 2%). Seven percent of males and 17% of females appeared as both a suspect and a victim in later police reports. There also were significant gender differences in the frequency of suspect (χ^2 = 119.3, df = 2, p < .001) and victim recidivism (χ^2 = 815.1, df = 2, p < .001). Males were more likely to recidivate as a suspect in two or more incidents (26% vs. 11%) and females were more likely to be a victim in two or more subsequent incidents (25% vs. 2%). In Portland, as in Memphis, a small percentage of female DV offenders recidivated as suspects only (8%) and some were repeat suspects. By adding the percentage of women who recidivated as suspect only (8%) with the percentage that recidivated as both a suspect and victim (17%), a quarter of female DV suspects were deemed aggressors in future intimate partner violence. This percentage of female aggressors is compatible with other research findings and DV arrest statistics, and suggests the perception of female DV suspects as victims only requires clarification and further systematic inquiry (Conradi, 2004; Henning & Feder, 2004; Henning & Renauer, under review; Martin, 1997; Miller, 2001; Swan & Snow, 2002).

The preceding analyses suggest that male and female DV offenders recidivate in different ways: the former are more likely to perpetrate new offenses while the latter are more likely to be victimized during later DV incidents. These conclusions are limited, however, by the fact that the male and female offenders were demographically different (e.g., age and victim-offender relationship in Memphis and age and race in Portland). These dissimilarities might account for the variable recidivism rates observed as a function of gender. Four logistic regression models were run, therefore, to assess the independent association between gender and recidivism. Gender and the demographic characteristics available from each site were entered simultaneously as predictor variables in these analyses. The two criterion variables used in each sample were (1) recidivism as a suspect (i.e., any new report), and (2) recidivism as a victim. Table 3 provides the results of these regressions. The findings indicate that gender, independent of other factors, was reliably associated with both recidivism as suspect (p = < .05 in Memphis, p = < .001 in Portland) and victim (p = < .001 in Memphis, p = < .001 in Portland). Specifically, being male significantly increased the odds of recidivism as a suspect (odds ratio of 3.2 for Memphis and 2.5 for Portland) and significantly decreased the odds of recidivism as a victim (.22 and .13, respectively).

☐ **Table 3: Simultaneous Logistic Regression Models Predicting Domestic Violence Recidivism in Portland and Memphis Samples**

	Sample							
	Recidivism in Memphis				Recidivism in Portland			
	As Suspect		As Victim		As Suspect		As Victim	
	B	Odds	B	Odds	B	Odds	B	Odds
Offender Characteristics								
Gender (male)	1.16	3.20***	−1.52	.22***	.92	2.50***	−2.06	.13***
Age (years)	−.02	.98**	−.02	.98*	−.01	.99*	.01	1.01*
Race (minority)	.44	1.55*	.17	1.18	.39	1.48***	.42	1.52***
Relationship to Victim (dating)	.07	1.08	.26	1.29				
Model								
N	880		880		6,010		6,010	
−2 Log Likelihood	994.0		897.5		8,050.4		4,135.1	
χ^2	70.7***		92.3***		178.7***		481.5***	

*$p < .05$ **$p < .01$ ***$p < .001$

DISCUSSION

The present study sought to address an important and yet largely ignored question in the field of DV: who is more likely to recidivate, male or female DV offenders involved with the criminal justice system? Recent increases in the number of people charged with assaulting an intimate partner have taxed criminal justice resources in many jurisdictions and led to efforts to prioritize cases based on the offender's potential for future violence and/or lethal assaults. Virtually all of the risk assessment scales developed for this purpose have been designed for use with male offenders. Nevertheless, women account for a significant and increasing proportion of those charged with DV crimes. Victim advocates and some family violence researchers have argued that most of these women are victims of abuse who were arrested for acts of self-defense (Chesney-Lind, 2002; McMahon & Pence, 2003; Miller, 2001; Saunders, 1995). As such, we would not expect to see high numbers of these women recidivate as a suspect in later DV incidents. Instead, they would be more likely to show up as a victim in later offenses perpetrated by their spouse/partner.

Other researchers have found that there is greater heterogeneity among the women cited for DV offenses than has been previously recognized. Henning and Renauer (under review) discovered that roughly one in ten women who were found guilty of assaulting an intimate partner self-reported being the primary aggressor in their relationship. Another group of women, accounting for about a third of the sample, reported that they perpetrated a similar level of aggression against their spouse/partner as they received in return. Comparable findings have been reported in other studies (e.g., Conradi, 2004; Swan & Snow, 2002), raising the possibility that some female offenders are at risk to recidivate with new offenses against their intimate partners.

The results of the present study provide support for both of these hypotheses. First, the female DV offenders as a group were significantly less likely than male offenders to recidivate as a suspect and fewer women had multiple new offenses. When the women did show up again in subsequent DV reports it was more commonly as a victim. This pattern of results suggests that many of the women who were cited by the police as suspects were the primary victim of the aggression in their relationship. The police officers who responded to the instant offense, whether through lack of training, poor information, manipulation by the male batterer, or some form of personal or institutional bias, failed to correctly identify the male as the aggressor. Criminalizing these female victims for possible acts of self-defense could lead to a number of negative consequences including the loss of access to victim services, financial instability, increased vulnerability to their abusive spouse/partner, and a reluctance to rely upon the criminal justice system for assistance (Crager, Cousin, & Hardy, 2003; Miller, 2001; Hirschel & Buzawa, 2002). Efforts to avert these repercussions need to center upon the accurate identification of the primary aggressor by first response officers. Additional DV training for law enforcement, timely access to information in the field (e.g., prior 911 calls, criminal histories of both parties), and legislation that requires officers to identify and arrest only the primary aggressor from each incident are suggested components of an effective response to this dilemma (Dasgupta, 2002; Martin, 1997; McMahon & Pence, 2003; Miller, 2001). Strict departmental policies regarding the use of dual arrest and the identification of the primary aggressor also may reduce the number of female victims labeled by officers as suspects (Finn, Blackwell, Stalans, Studdard, & Dugan, 2004).

While concern over treating victims as suspects is certainly justified given the possible negative consequences, the present findings also show that not all female DV offenders fit the profile of an abused woman who was caught a single time for fighting back in self-defense. Six percent of the female offenders in Memphis and 8% of those from Portland were listed as a "pure suspect" in later police reports: they committed one or more new DV offenses in the absence of reports identifying them as a victim. Prior studies using self-reported data have suggested a similar percent of female DV offenders might be classified as the primary aggressor in their intimate relationship (Conradi, 2004; Henning & Renauer, under review; Swan & Snow, 2002).

Although it appears that fewer than one in ten of the women in our samples were pure suspects, this number may be underestimated due to a possible gender bias in officer's decisions regarding the labeling of suspects. Departmental policies and trainings that define DV as a gendered crime may lead officers to assume that males are usually the aggressors in conflicts between intimate partners. Although this may be true for the majority of cases, there are undoubtedly times when the primary offender cannot be easily identified (e.g., both individuals are injured and blame each other for the offense). If officers typically resolve these situations by labeling the male as the suspect then rates of recidivism for men would be artificially inflated while rates for women would be decreased.

Direct research on this issue could not be found in the literature, but two related studies support the conclusion that there may be a gender bias that occurs when attributing blame for DV incidents. Finn and Stalans (1997) varied the gender of the victim and offender in DV narratives and found that police officers reading these reports attributed greater blame for the incident to male victims than female victims. This in turn influenced whether the officers would have made an arrest in the given situation. Harris and Cook (1994) found that college students had a similar bias: Greater responsibility was placed on the victim in narratives portraying a male victim compared to a female victim and the former incidents were seen as less serious by the students even though the only factor that differed was gender. These studies and others that find women are treated more leniently by the criminal justice system (e.g., Spohn & Biechner, 2000) suggest that police officers may have greater difficulty assigning women blame for offenses involving intimate partners, even in cases where this might be appropriate.

Women who are the primary aggressors in their relationships, like their male counterparts, may be using aggression for instrumental purposes and/or have limited skills for resolving relationship conflicts using nonviolent means. Rather than treat these women as victims, it may be best to require that they participate in programs that challenge their attitudes about violence, teach conflict resolution skills, and reduce cognitive distortions that support their aggressive behavior. Further research is also needed to understand the impact of the aggression committed by these women. Research with female DV victims indicates an increased risk for post-traumatic stress disorder (PTSD), depression, substance abuse, and other psychological difficulties (Golding, 1999; Holtzworth-Munroe, Smutzler, & Sandin, 1997; Jones, Hughes, & Unterstaller, 2001). The extent to which male victims experience similar problems as a result of actions perpetrated by their spouse/partner remains unclear. Similarly, children often witness marital violence (e.g., Fantuzzo, Boruch, Beriama, Atkins, & Marcus, 1997) and studies indicate that short-term and long-term maladjustment may result from such exposure (Jaffe, Wolfe, & Wilson, 1990; Kitzmann, Gaylord, Holt, & Kenny, 2003; Mohr, Noone-Lutz, Fantuzzo, & Perry, 2000). Virtually all of this research has focused on paternal to maternal aggression, highlighting a need for studies on the impact of witnessing intimate partner violence perpetrated by mothers.

The present study also identified a third group of women, those who show up in later reports as both a victim and suspect (12% in Memphis, 17% in Portland). This dual recidivism among some females (and males for that matter) could be an indicator of mutual aggression similar to Johnson's (1995) notion of Common Couple Violence (CCV). Johnson theorized that CCV involves aggression that is of low severity and frequency, usually bidirectional, and rarely does it lead to a pattern of escalating violence over time. By contrast, Intimate Terrorism (IT) involves severe violence and abuse usually perpetrated by men with the aim of controlling their female intimate partner. While Johnson (1995) originally proposed that CCV is rare in criminal justice settings, he suggested these cases more commonly involve male perpetrated IT, recent implementation of mandatory and pro-arrest laws may have led to increased arrests among men and women who engage in CCV. The bidirectional nature of this form of DV presents a challenge to criminal justice professionals and treatment providers who are more accustomed to dealing with clear-cut victims and offenders. District attorneys appear to respond to these ambiguous cases by dismissing the charges at higher rates compared to other defendants (e.g., Henning & Feder, in press). Treatment providers who work with court-ordered offenders are in a more difficult position when dealing with CCV in that few programs have been developed to address mutual aggression. Indeed, some states have passed legislation that prevents clinicians from using marital/conjoint therapy altogether on the grounds that it endangers the women and excuses the male's violence (Holtzworth-Munroe, 2002; O'Leary, 2002). An alternative to this perspective is that higher recidivism rates, including further offenses against the women, may result from failing to address the systemic nature of the aggression within this small number of mutually aggressive couples (Straus, 2005).

Implications for DV Risk Assessment

Notwithstanding the limitations noted previously, the present study has implications for risk assessment with DV offenders. Female offenders in both of the samples tested were significantly less likely to recidivate as suspects compared to male offenders. Similar results are reported in the only other published study addressing gender as a factor in DV recidivism (Wooldredge & Thistlethwaite, 2002) and the findings are consistent with gender differences in the general recidivism literature, where males are more likely to recidivate than females (Gendreau, Little, & Goggin, 1996; Jones & Sims, 1997; Langan & Levin, 2002). It follows, therefore, that gender should be considered as a risk factor when evaluating DV offenders. In the absence of other overriding factors, police officers might be justified if they were to take gender into account while making arrest decisions.[3] Similarly, the informal policies established by some police departments and district attorneys to prioritize cases involving male offenders are supported by the present study in that men are indeed more likely to reoffend compared to their female counterparts. As for community supervision and treatment programming, the broader literature on effective correctional interventions suggests that high-risk offenders should receive the most intense services (Andrews, Zinger, Hoge, Bonta, Gendreau, & Cullen, 1990). Thus, male DV offenders should continue to be the priority for probation officers and mental health counselors.

Although gender should be considered as a risk factor, it does not necessarily follow that this item simply be added to existing scales used to evaluate DV offenders. All of the measures presented in the literature with supporting validity data were developed exclusively with male samples (e.g., Campbell et al., 2003; Hilton et al., 2004; Kropp et al., 1998). The factors that predict recidivism may differ by gender, especially if male and female DV offenders are dissimilar in other regards. In the present study, a type of female offender who is both a victim and a suspect was identified, a profile that was much less common among male offenders. Similarly, Henning and Feder (2004) and Henning,

Jones, and Holdford (2003) found numerous differences between male and female DV offenders when they examined their demographic profiles, psychological functioning, and criminal histories. Thus, a "unisex" DV risk scale may not be appropriate and separate measures for male and female offenders need to be considered.

Lastly, the phenomenon of mutual aggression or CCV (Johnson, 1995) presents a challenge to the developers of risk assessment instruments. The bidirectional nature of some DV raises the question of whether evaluators should consider characteristics of both partners. Traditionally, forensic risk assessments have focused on the identification of offender characteristics that are correlated with recidivism. For many crimes like robbery, rape, aggravated assault, and property offenses the offender usually does not have continued contact with the victim after the instant offense. Thus, the victim's characteristics are unlikely to influence whether the given offender recidivates. Domestic violence, which involves a complex pre-existing relationship between the two people that often continues even after legal intervention, is an exception to this general rule. It is possible that the demographic, psychological, and behavioral characteristics of both parties predict whether a subsequent offense occurs. Further research is clearly needed to evaluate this possibility.

Data Limitations and Strengths

A major limitation of the present study that raises serious questions about the results and conclusions derived previously is that recidivism was based solely on police reports. Many DV incidents are never reported to the police (Greenfeld, Craven, Klaus, Perkins, Ringel, Warchol, Matson, & Fox, 1998), leading to an underestimation of recidivism for both male and female DV offenders in the present samples. This would be of greater concern, however, if rates of reporting differed as a function of the victim's gender. Data from the 1998 National Crime Victimization Survey (NCVS: Rennison & Welchans, 2000) indicate that women were slightly more likely than men to report assaults by an intimate partner to the police (53% vs. 46%), but this difference was not statistically reliable. Whether men are less likely to report DV victimization to NCVS interviewers and other survey researchers remains unknown, although this has been suggested by some men's advocacy groups.

A second problem with the use of police reports to determine DV recidivism is that responding officers typically identify only one individual as the suspect and the other as the victim.[4] These polarized labels do not always accurately reflect each individual's involvement in the conflict. As noted previously, some of the aggression that occurs in intimate relationships appears to be bidirectional (Johnson, 1995; Straus, 2005) and it may be difficult if not impossible to identify the primary instigator. Nevertheless, in some police reports the woman (or man) is labeled the "victim" simply because her own injuries were slightly more serious than those of her partner. Likewise, the person who used the more dangerous weapon might be identified as the "suspect" even though both parties were armed during the conflict. The timing of each person's aggression could influence who is designated as the suspect as well: Officers are probably more likely to base their decisions on aggressive actions that they directly witness rather than trust reports of what happened prior to their arrival. In short, some "victims" may have done things to precipitate their partner's aggression and other victims were labeled as such simply because their own behavior was slightly less serious than that of their intimate partner. This becomes a problem for recidivism studies because researchers are interested in predicting whether individuals continue engaging in inappropriate behavior; it is still important even if someone was only 49% responsible for a domestic dispute with their partner (and thereby listed as the victim). Thus, future studies need to look beyond the labels applied by the police during new offenses and study whether there are gender differences in things like injuries caused, the use of weapons, property damage, involvement of the children, and psychological harm to each person involved.

An equally concerning problem regarding the use of police data is that anecdotal evidence suggests that some male batterers have learned to manipulate the criminal justice system and their spouse/partner by falsely reporting DV incidents (Miller, 2001). Officers responding to 911 are instructed to identify the role of each person involved in an incident (e.g., suspect, victim), a process that is likely influenced by the identity of the original complainant. Thus, higher rates of recidivism may have been found among the female offenders than might really be the case. This bias could work both ways, however, with some of the complaints filed by female victims being motivated by other purposes (e.g., retaliation, evidence for child custody disputes). Indeed, research with female DV offenders suggests that they engage in a similar level of minimization and denial as male offenders (Henning, Jones, & Holdford, in press).

Several strengths of the present study are worth mentioning following this discussion of limitations. The sample sizes employed were quite large compared to most DV recidivism studies, leading to greater confidence in the stability of the findings. Similarly, the fact that data from two demographically different cities yielded virtually the same patterns adds to the generalizability of the results. Lengthy follow-up periods and efforts to control for other factors that might have accounted for the gender differences observed are additional merits of this research.

NOTES

1. The term "offender" is used throughout the paper to describe men and women who have been identified as suspects in DV reports by police. We recognize that the term may be inappropriate in some cases (e.g., women arrested for self-defense, suspects who were later cleared of committing any crime); however, we also believe that consistent use of the term facilitates reading of the paper.

2. By law Memphis and Portland police officers have to make an official report of any domestic violence incident regardless of arrest. Arrest data files were not available to us. Based on police report narratives in Memphis, roughly half of the DV suspects in Memphis were not on site for arrest when police arrived.

3. As noted previously, a limitation of recidivism data like that used in the present study is that officers may already consider gender as a risk factor when deciding who to arrest. While this presents a significant challenge to researchers, it makes sense from a practitioner's perspective.

4. While officers occasionally make dual arrests in these situations, the use of dual arrest varies dramatically across jurisdictions (Hirschel & Buzawa, 2002). Moreover, officers appear to be influenced by perceptions of their department's support for such arrests. Finn and colleagues (2004) presented police officers with a hypothetical script where both the husband and wife were injured during a domestic dispute. Officers who perceived that their department supported dual arrests were more likely to use this option. Those who believed their department was interested in arresting only the primary aggressor were more likely to arrest just the husband.

REFERENCES

Aldridge, M., & Browne, K. (2003). Perpetrators of spousal homicide: A review. *Trauma Violence & Abuse, 4(3)*, 265-276.

Andrews, D., Zinger, I., Hoge, R., Bonta, J., Gendreau, P., & Cullen, F. (1990). Does correctional treatment work? A psychologically informed meta-analysis. *Criminology, 28(3)*, 369-404.

Archer, J. (2000). Sex differences in aggression between heterosexual partners: A meta-analytic review. *Psychological Bulletin, 126(5)*, 651-680.

Campbell, J. C. (1995). Prediction of homicide of and by battered women. In J. C. Campbell (Ed.), Assessing dangerousness: Violence by sexual offenders, batterers, and child abusers (pp. 96-113). Thousand Oaks, CA: Sage.

Campbell, J., Webster, D., Koziol-McLain, J., Block, C., Campbell, D., Gary, F., McFarlane, J., Sachs, C., Sharps, P., Ulrich, Y., Wilt, S., Manganello, J., Xu, X., Schollenberger, J., & Frye, V. (2003). Risk factors for femicide in abusive relationships: Results from a multisite case control study. *American Journal of Public Health, 93,* 1089-1097.

Cascardi, M., & Vivian, D. (1995). Context for specific episodes of marital violence: Gender and severity of violence differences. *Journal of Family Violence, 10(3),* 265-293.

Chesney-Lind, M. (2002). Criminalizing victimization: The unintended consequences of pro-arrest policies for girls and women. *Criminology & Public Policy, 2(1),* 81-90.

Conradi, L. (2004, September). *An exploratory study of heterosexual females as dominant aggressors of physical violence in their intimate relationships.* Paper presented at the 9th International Conference on Family Violence, San Diego, CA.

Crager, M., Cousin, M., & Hardy, T. (2003). *Victim-defendants: An emerging challenge in responding to domestic violence in Seattle and the King County region.* King County Coalition Against Domestic Violence.

Dasgupta, S. (2002). A framework for understanding women's use of nonlethal violence in intimate heterosexual relationships. *Violence Against Women, 8(11),* 1364-1389.

Dutton, D., & Kropp, R. (2000). A review of domestic violence risk instruments. *Trauma, Violence, & Abuse, 1(2),* 171-181.

Eigenberg, H., Scarborough, K., & Kappeler, V. (1996). Contributory factors affecting arrest in domestic and non-domestic assaults. *American Journal of Police, 15(4),* 27-54.

Fagan, J. (1996). *The criminalization of domestic violence: Promises and limits* (NCJ 157641). Washington, DC: Office of Justice Programs.

Fantuzzo, J., Boruch, R., Beriama, A., Atkins, M., & Marcus, S. (1997). Domestic violence and children: Prevalence and risk in five major U.S. cities. *Journal of the American Academy of Child and Adolescent Psychiatry, 36(1),* 116-122.

Ferraro, K. (1989). Policing woman battering. *Social Problems, 36(1),* 61-74.

Finn, M., & Stalans, L. (1997). The influence of gender and mental state on police decisions in domestic assault cases. *Criminal Justice & Behavior, 24(2),* 157-176.

Finn, M., Blackwell, B., & Stalans, L., Studdard, S., & Dugan, L. (2004). Dual arrest decisions in domestic violence cases: The influence of departmental policies. *Crime & Delinquency, 50(4),* 565-589.

Ford, D. (1993). *The Indianapolis domestic violence prosecution experiment–final report.* Washington, DC: National Institute of Justice.

Gelles, R., & Tolman, R. (1998). *The Kingston Screening Instrument for Domestic Violence (KSID).* Unpublished risk instrument, University of Rhode Island, Providence.

Gendreau, P., Little, T., & Goggin, C. (1996). A meta-analysis of the predictors of adult offender recidivism: What works? *Criminology, 34(4),* 575-607.

Golding, J. M. (1999). Intimate partner violence as a risk factor for mental disorders: A meta-analysis. *Journal of Family Violence, 14,* 99-133.

Gondolf, E. (1997). Batterer programs: What we know and need to know. *Journal of Interpersonal Violence, 12(1)*, 83-98.

Grann, M., & Wedin, I. (2002). Risk factors for recidivism among spousal assault and spousal homicide offenders. *Psychology, Crime & Law, 8*, 5-23.

Greenfeld, L., Craven, D., Klaus, P., Perkins, C., Ringel, C., Warchol, G., Matson, C., & Fox, J. A. (1998). *Violence by intimates: Analysis of data on crimes by current or former spouses, boyfriends and girlfriends* (NCJ 167237). Washington, DC: US Department of Justice, Bureau of Justice Statistics.

Grove, W., & Meehl, P. (1996). Comparative efficiency of informal (subjective, impressionistic) and formal (mechanical, algorithmic) prediction procedures: The clinical-statistical controversy. *Psychology, Public Policy, and Law, 2*, 293-323.

Hamberger, L. K., & Potente, T. (1994). Counseling heterosexual women arrested for domestic violence: Implications for theory and practice. *Violence & Victims, 9(2)*, 125-137.

Harris, R., & Cook, C. (1994). Attributions about spouse abuse: It matters who the batterers and victims are. *Sex Roles, 30(7-8)*, 553-565.

Henning, K., & Feder, L. (2004). A comparison between men and women arrested for domestic violence: Who presents the greater threat? *Journal of Family Violence, 19(2)*, 69-80.

Henning, K., & Feder, L. (in press). Criminal prosecution of domestic violence offenses: An investigation of factors predictive of court outcomes. *Criminal Justice and Behavior.*

Henning, K., Jones, A., & Holdford, R. (2003). Treatment needs of women arrested for domestic violence: A comparison with male offenders. *Journal of Interpersonal Violence, 8(8)*, 839-856.

Henning, K., Jones, A., & Holdford, R. (in press). "I didn't do it, but if I did I had a good reason": Minimization, denial, and attributions of blame among male and female domestic violence offenders. *Journal of Family Violence.*

Henning, K., & Renauer, B. (Under review) Victim or offender? Heterogeneity among women arrested for intimate partner violence. *Journal of Aggression, Maltreatment, and Trauma.*

Henning, K., & Renauer, B. (in press). Prosecution of women arrested for domestic violence: Are they treated more leniently than men? *Violence and Victims.*

Hilton, N., Harris, G., Rice, M., Lang, C., Cormier, C., & Lines, K. (2004). A brief actuarial assessment for the prediction of wife assault recidivism: The Ontario Domestic Assault Risk Assessment. *Psychological Assessment, 16*, 300-312.

Hirschel, D., & Buzawa, E. (2002). Understanding the context of dual arrest with directions for future research. *Violence Against Women, 8(12)*, 1449-1473.

Holtzworth-Munroe, A. (2002). Standards for batterer treatment programs: How can research inform our decisions? *Journal of Aggression, Maltreatment & Trauma, 5(2)*, 165-180.

Holtzworth-Munroe, A., Smutzler, N., & Sandin, E. (1997). A brief review of the research on husband violence: The psychological effects of husband violence on battered women and their children. *Aggression and Violent Behavior, 2(2)*, 179-213.

Jaffe, P., Wolfe, D., & Wilson, S. (1990). *Children of battered women.* Newbury Park, CA: Sage.

Johnson, M. (1995). Patriarchal terrorism and common couple violence: Two forms of violence against women. *Journal of Marriage & the Family, 57(2)*, 283-294.

Jones, M., & Sims, B. (1997). Recidivism of offenders released from prison in North Carolina: A gender comparison. *The Prison Journal, 77(3)*, 335-348.

Jones, L., Hughes, M., & Unterstaller, U. (2001). Post-traumatic Stress Disorder (PTSD) in victims of domestic violence: A review of the research. *Trauma, Violence, & Abuse, 2(2)*, 99-119.

Kane, R. J. (2000). Police responses to restraining orders in domestic violence incidents: Identifying the custody-threshold thesis. *Criminal Justice & Behavior, 27(5)*, 561-580.

Kitzmann, K., Gaylord, N., Holt, A., & Kenny, E. (2003). Child witnesses to domestic violence: A meta-analytic review. *Journal of Consulting and Clinical Psychology, 71(2)*, 339-352.

Kropp, P., (2004). Some questions regarding spousal assault risk assessment. *Violence Against Women, 10(6)*, 676-697.

Kropp, P. Hart, S., Webster, C., & Eaves, D. (1998). *Spousal Assault Risk Assessment: User's guide*. Toronto, Canada: Multi-Health Systems.

Langan, P., & Levin, D. (2002). *Recidivism of prisoners released in 1994* (NCJ 193427). Washington, DC: US Department of Justice, Bureau of Justice Statistics.

Loseke, D., & Kurz, D. (2005). Men's violence toward women. In D. Loseke, R. Gelles, & M. Cavanaugh (Eds.), *Current controversies on family violence* (pp. 79-95). Thousand Oaks, CA: Sage.

Martin, M. (1997). Double your trouble: Dual arrest in family violence. *Journal of Family Violence, 12(2)*, 139-157.

Maxwell, C., Garner, J., & Fagan, J. (2001). *The effects of arrest on intimate partner violence: New evidence from the Spouse Assault Replication Program* (NCJ 188199). Washington, DC: US Department of Justice.

McMahon, M., & Pence, E. (2003). Making social change: Reflections on individual and institutional advocacy with women arrested for domestic violence. *Violence Against Women, 9(1)*, 47-74.

McNeely, R., Cook, P., & Torres, J. (2001). Is domestic violence a gender issue, or a human issue? *Journal of Human Behavior in the Social Environment, 4(4)*, 227-251.

Mignon, S., & Holmes, W. (1995). Police response to mandatory arrest laws. *Crime & Delinquency, 41(4)*, 430-443.

Miller, N. (1998, June). *Domestic violence legislation affecting police and prosecutor responsibilities in the United States: Inferences from a 50-state review of state statutory codes*. Presentation to the 5th International Family Violence Conference University of New Hampshire.

Miller, S. (2001). The paradox of women arrested for domestic violence: Criminal justice professionals and service providers respond. *Violence Against Women, 7(12)*, 1339-1376.

Mohr, W., Noone-Lutz, M., Fantuzzo, J., & Perry, M. (2000). Children exposed to family violence: A review of empirical research from a developmental-ecological perspective. *Trauma, Violence, & Abuse, 1(3)*, 264-283.

Moracco, K., Runyan, C., & Butts, J. (1998). Femicide in North Carolina, 1991-1993: A statewide study of patterns and precursors. *Homicide Studies, 2*, 422-446.

O'Leary, K. D. (2002). Conjoint therapy for partners who engage in physically aggressive behavior: Rationale and research. *Journal of Aggression, Maltreatment & Trauma, 5(2),* 145-164.

Olson, D., Alderden, M., & Lurigio, A. (2003). Men are from Mars and women are from Venus, but what role does gender play in probation recidivism? *Justice Research and Police, 5(2),* 33-54.

Quinsey, V., Harris, G., Rice, M., & Cormier, C. (1998). *Violent offenders: Appraising and managing risk.* Washington, DC: American Psychological Association.

Rauma, D. (1984). Going for the gold: Prosecutorial decision making in cases of wife assault. *Social Science Research, 13,* 321-51.

Rennison, C., & Welchens, S. (2000) *Intimate partner violence* (NCJ 178247). Washington, DC: US Department of Justice, Bureau of Justice Statistics.

Roehl, J., & Guertin, K. (2000). Intimate partner violence: The current use of risk assessments in sentencing offenders. *The Justice System Journal, 21,* 171-198.

Saunders, D. (1995). *Prediction of wife assault.* In J. Campbell (Ed.), Assessing dangerousness: Violence by sexual offenders, batterers, and child abusers (pp. 173-196). Thousand Oaks, CA: Sage.

Saunders, D. (2002). Are physical assault by wives and girlfriends a major social problem? *Violence Against Women, 8(12),* 1424-1448.

Schmidt, J., & Steury, E. (1989). Prosecutorial discretion in filing charges in domestic violence cases. *Criminology, 27,* 487-510.

Sherman, L., & Cohn, E. (1989). The impact of research on legal policy: The Minneapolis Domestic Violence Experiment. *Law & Society Review, 23(1),* 117-144.

Sherman, L. (1992). *Policing domestic violence: Experiments and dilemmas.* New York: Free Press.

Smith, D., & Klein, J. (1984). Police control of interpersonal disputes. *Social Problems, 31(4),* 468-481.

Smith, D. (1987). Police response to interpersonal violence: Defining the parameters of legal control. *Social Forces, 65(3),* 767-782.

Spohn, C., & Beichner, D. (2000). Is preferential treatment of female offenders a thing of the past? A multisite study of gender, race, and imprisonment. *Criminal Justice Policy Review, 11(2),* 149-184.

Straus, M. (2005). Women's violence toward men. In D. Loseke, R. Gelles, & M. Cavanaugh (Eds.), *Current controversies on family violence* (pp. 55-77). Thousand Oaks, CA: Sage.

Swan, S., & Snow, D. (2002). A typology of women's use of violence in intimate relationships. *Violence Against Women, 8(3),* 286-319.

Tjaden, P., & Thoennes, N. (2000). Prevalence and consequences of male-to-female and female-to-male intimate partner violence as measured by the National Violence Against Women Survey. *Violence Against Women, 6(2),* 142-161.

Victim Services Agency (1989). State legislation providing for law enforcement response to family violence. *Response, 12(3),* 6-9.

Wooldredge, J., & Thistlethwaite, A. (2002). Reconsidering domestic violence recidivism: Conditioned effects of legal control by individual and aggregate levels of stake in conformity. *Journal of Quantitative Criminology, 18*(1), 45-70.

AUTHORS' NOTES

Brian Renauer, PhD, is Assistant Professor in criminology and criminal justice at Portland State University. His current research interests include the police and prosecutorial response to domestic violence and urban neighborhoods and crime.

Kris Henning, PhD, is Associate Professor in criminology and criminal justice at Portland State University. His current research focuses on domestic violence, including studies on risk assessment with male batterers, the use of prosecutorial discretion, and women arrested for intimate partner abuse.

This research could not have been done without the support of officers and command staff in the Memphis Police Department and the Portland Police Bureau; the authors offer thanks for trusting them with these data. The authors would like to thank James White and Hallie Kilbert from Portland State University for their assistance in coding the data.

Address correspondence to Brian Renauer, P.O Box 751-JUST, Criminology and Criminal Justice, Portland State University, Portland, OR 97207 (E-mail: renauer@ pdx.edu).

Index